WRITING PATHWAYS TO STUDENT SUCCESS

PRACTICE AND PEDAGOGY

Series Editor: Mike Palmquist

The Practice & Pedagogy series addresses the teaching, learning, and practice of writing in all its forms. From Joseph Williams' reflections on introductions to Richard E. Young's taxonomy of "small genres" to Adam Mackie's considerations of technology, the books in this occasional series explore issues and ideas of interest to writers and teachers of writing.

The WAC Clearinghouse, Colorado State University Open Press, and University Press of Colorado are collaborating so that these books will be widely available through free digital distribution and low-cost print editions. The publishers and the Series editor are committed to the principle that knowledge should freely circulate. We see the opportunities that new technologies have for further democratizing knowledge. And we see that to share the power of writing is to share the means for all to articulate their needs, interest, and learning into the great experiment of literacy.

OTHER BOOKS IN THE SERIES

Charles Bazerman, *Involved: Writing for College, Writing for Your Self* (2015)

Adam Mackie, *New Literacies Dictionary: Primer for the Twenty-first Century Learner* (2011)

Patricia A. Dunn, *Learning Re-abled: The Learning Disability Controversy and Composition Studies* (2011)

Richard E. Young, *Toward A Taxonomy of "Small" Genres and Writing Techniques for Writing Across the Curriculum* (2011)

Joseph M. Williams, *Problems into PROBLEMS: A Rhetoric of Motivation* (2011)

Charles Bazerman, *The Informed Writer: Using Sources in the Disciplines* (2011)

WRITING PATHWAYS TO STUDENT SUCCESS

Edited by Lillian Craton, Renée Love, and Sean Barnette

The WAC Clearinghouse
wac.colostate.edu
Fort Collins, Colorado

University Press of Colorado
upcolorado.com
Louisville, Colorado

The WAC Clearinghouse, Fort Collins, Colorado 80523–1040

University Press of Colorado, Louisville, Colorado 80027

Printed in the United States of America

Names: Craton, Lillian, editor. | Love, Renée, 1969– editor. | Barnette, Sean, editor.
Title: Writing pathways to student success / edited by Lillian Craton, Renée Love, and Sean Barnette.
Description: Fort Collins, Colorado : The WAC Clearinghouse ; Boulder, Colorado : University Press of Colorado, [2017] | Includes bibliographical references and index.
Identifiers: LCCN 2017034929| ISBN 9781607327691 (pbk.) | ISBN 9781607327707 (ebook)
Subjects: LCSH: English language—Rhetoric—Study and teaching (Higher) | Life skills—Study and teaching. | Academic achievement.
Classification: LCC PE1404 .W7293 2017 | DDC 808/.0420711—dc23
LC record available at https://lccn.loc.gov/2017034929

Copyeditor: Brandy Bippes
Designer: Mike Palmquist
Cover: Design by Malcolm Childers, photograph by Mike Palmquist
Series Editor: Mike Palmquist

The WAC Clearinghouse supports teachers of writing across the disciplines. Hosted by Colorado State University, and supported by the Colorado State Univeristy Open Press, it brings together scholarly journals and book series as well as resources for teachers who use writing in their courses. This book is available in digital formats for free download at wac.colostate.edu.

Founded in 1965, the University Press of Colorado is a nonprofit cooperative publishing enterprise supported, in part, by Adams State University, Colorado State University, Fort Lewis College, Metropolitan State University of Denver, Regis University, University of Colorado, University of Northern Colorado, Utah State University, and Western State Colorado University. For more information, visit upcolorado.com.

Contents

Preface

Teachers of first-year composition courses do essential work, as do those who teach writing in every discipline. We teach argumentation and conventions of university-level writing; we demystify citation and punctuation; we promote reading comprehension and analysis. Yet such skills, as important as they are, do not reflect the full impact of writing instruction. Every year we shepherd a flock of new college students through their initial semesters of higher education as they acquire a host of *hard* and *soft* skills essential to college and professional careers. This book is an examination of life lessons that students and instructors learn from writing courses.

Some of the most meaningful outcomes of writing coursework relate to students' growth as successful individuals able to live and write in a complex world. Writing instructors demand civil discourse and respect for diversity. We coach students in time management and the creative process. We build up confidence, break down learning obstacles, and promote self-examination. The lessons about human experience students learn in English 101 can be hard to explain, but these lessons are no less important than teaching students about academic discourse. In a challenging economic climate, all stakeholders—students, their families, university administrators, faculty members—want good reasons to invest in higher education. Students need writing, rhetoric, and language instruction for future college courses and professional careers. However, real success also demands a range of subtle abilities like tolerance, self-discipline, intellectual complexity, ability to connect, and emotional intelligence.

Writing instructors have a remarkable opportunity to shape the attitudes and behaviors that guide students to success, but that opportunity can be tricky. On one hand, writing faculty often have the clearest perspective on students' lifestyles and habits of thought—many students are astoundingly candid in their written work—and thus these writing faculty have the best chance of promoting healthy academic and personal behaviors. Our students may need help understanding their roles in the classroom before they can achieve academic goals. When they are in crisis, we are often the first to know. Yet, generally speaking, we are neither students' parents nor trained therapists; we are blatantly unqualified to solve many of our students' problems. We also have a rich body of core material that students must master, so we have little time to spare. If we are to address extra-disciplinary issues of growth and behavior in the classroom, we must do so ethically and mindfully of our core task to teach good writing.

This book gathers diverse perspectives on three questions: Why We Write, How We Write, and What We Write. The first section, Why We Write, offers perspectives on the importance of rhetoric and self-expression for students' ability to thrive in and after college. These chapters look at the academic, professional, and social value that the study of writing creates for students. The second, How We Write, reflects on how we might incorporate practices from other disciplines into writing pedagogy, including practices from studio art, theatre, and dance; further, writing teachers discuss how incorporating a holistic, affective pedagogy and team teaching and mentoring practices can benefit both students and teachers. The third, What We Write, explores specific writing topics and writing-instruction techniques that promote broad-based student learning. These chapters include consideration of how and whether to depend on technology through examination of high- and low-tech writing assignments, as well as some other writing projects that create important learning for the professional and personal lives of students. Throughout, the collection embraces traditional and current themes in the scholarship of composition and rhetoric; we strived to find a Janus-faced approach, blending pedagogical practices with philosophical questions that may lead us to new paths.

In putting this collection together, we have been grateful for the professionalism and inspiration of our contributors. They draw on their expertise as teachers and scholars in a wide range of higher education settings, from community colleges to liberal arts institutions to historically black colleges to flagship universities. Their diversity of perspectives enriches the collection by illuminating the myriad pathways that writing creates to student success. This manuscript has benefited from the careful attention of three undergraduate editors from the English, education, and political science majors at Lander University: Brittany Faulkner, Joel Kurtz, and Ettele Toole. We are also grateful for the feedback of peer reviewers and the leadership of WAC Clearinghouse staff, particularly Dr. Mike Palmquist.

Lillian E. Craton
C. Renée Love
Sean Barnette
Autumn 2016

WRITING PATHWAYS TO STUDENT SUCCESS

Chapter 1. Introduction
Beyond Peanut Butter and Jelly

Sean Barnette

LANDER UNIVERSITY

I recently asked my first-year writing students to compose an analogy essay, explaining how writing is like something else. The analogies were revealing. Nearly all of my forty-five students across two sections chose to craft comparisons that highlighted the linear nature of the writing process: *Writing is like making a sandwich because first you have to set out your ingredients. Writing is like building a house because you have to begin with a blueprint. Writing is like tending a garden, and the first step is . . .* and so forth.

As we developed the essays in class, I prompted students to consider the limitations of analogies that highlighted only the linear steps in the writing process. What does one do with a sandwich, I asked them. What is a house for? Why do we plant gardens? It quickly became apparent that most of my students could not recall ever having been asked to articulate anything about writing beyond its formal qualities. Maybe in the best of times, my students seemed to believe, writing could be a means of expression (but not communication). But usually, school writing was merely a hoop to jump through: an exercise in understanding formal requirements, and too often just one more means of standardized assessment.

I don't believe that my students' views of school writing present an objective report on their previous writing classes, and I trust their high-school teachers continue to do good work in complicated and difficult circumstances. But I also suspect my students' views on school writing will not surprise any postsecondary teacher, and pervasiveness and persistence of those views underscores the need for writing teachers to be able to voice a vigorous and practical defense of why we teach writing. The essays in this first section attempt to do just that.

Whereas for most students (and some faculty, as well), the writing classroom is primarily a place to master the demands of school writing—a troublingly circular justification—the authors of these essays show that our writing courses have relevance for students' lives outside the classroom. Sarah Hardison O'Connor, for instance, points out how the rhetorical knowledge students develop in our classes can help them make sense of the informational chaos that surrounds them. As they do so, they develop an ability to comprehend and craft complex arguments, and consequently to act more critically and more powerfully as citizens. Karen Bishop Morris presents several ways that writing teachers might construct assignments to help students interact directly with the world outside the classroom. Such experiential learning, however, is valuable not only because of the bridge it builds from the classroom to the outside world, but also because of the academic benefits it fosters. As students participate in meaningful writing activities, Morris argues, they develop cultural capital essential to success at the university beyond the first-year writing course.

Of course, if the rhetorical training students get from us is to empower them to act in the real world, we as teachers should acknowledge that we share some responsibility for students' actions, however remote. Given the prevalence of violence in our local, national, and international communities, teachers can be understandably concerned when students write about violence. Nonetheless, drawing on FBI, US Secret Service, school threat assessment, and psychological research, Lori D. Brown suggests that violent texts are not to be feared or censored, but rather embraced, as they can offer opportunities for personal growth, improved student writing, and increased safety.

The final chapters of this section, essays by Rachel McCoppin and by Ruth A. Goldfine and Deborah Mixson-Brookshire, examine the effects that first-year writing assignments can have on students' values. One initial challenge for many students lies in recognizing that we each see the world from a particular point of view and that our audiences' perspectives may be quite different from our own. In her essay, McCoppin presents assignments that promote tolerance, empathy, and analysis of difference, and Goldfine and Mixson-Brookshire discuss how such assignments work—that is, the role that writing coursework plays in students' ethical development, and how argument analysis assignments can help students learn to formulate and articulate their individual perspectives.

Collectively, the essays in this section remind us why training in rhetoric was long considered indispensable to a meaningful education. It is true that writing classes train students in the skills they need to succeed in the short term, at the university. And it's also true that, like my students' analogical sandwich makers, writers need to have certain basic resources and abilities at our command in order to be successful, and given the competing demands on our time and our attention in writing classes, it might be that simple and safe is sometimes best. We could, in other words, get by on white bread and peanut butter and jelly, but without more ingredients than those at our fingertips, our creative options (not to mention our nutritional ones) remain limited. The ultimate value of our classes—the reason we write—lies in how they help our students make more creative and powerful use of the rhetorical resources available to them, and thus grow into more sophisticated, thoughtful, critical rhetorical agents.

Section 1: Why We Write

Chapter 2. A Confusion of Messages: The Critical Role of Rhetoric in the Information Age

Sarah Hardison O'Connor

James Madison University

The Latest Shiny Object

Chatter fills the airwaves about the latest technology: the e-reader, tablet, web TV, smart phone. Almost every day companies introduce some new hardware to bewilder carbon man. On top of that, platforms and applications multiply daily. Do you want to tweet, blog, text, podcast, webcast, Skype? Do you need an app to tell you how much you slept? To help you plan your Christmas shopping? *The Economist* magazine recently devoted 20 pages of prime real estate in the center of the magazine to a special report on personal technology titled "Beyond the PC." Nineteen of those pages discussed hardware and software innovations (Giles). A *New York Times* article tracked new digital gadgets just for children (Schmidt). Consumers want to know what is next. They are like crows swooping down on the latest shiny object to line their nests. Maybe it's time to be more concerned about the actual information we are receiving rather than the way in which we get it.

Until fairly recently, people got information from a limited number of sources—newspapers, radio, TV or books; today we access media from a multitude of sources. Much of what we find is unfiltered or hyped. Do students today, some of the heaviest users of technology, know how to evaluate information or analyze it? Do they know how to decide who or what is credible? Do they even know what questions to ask to make these kinds of judgments? It is time for anyone teaching in the field of higher education to find ways to incorporate basic principles of rhetoric into their teaching. Students in every discipline, from biology to political science to business, are using technology to access information and using that information in their research and writing. The ancient art of rhetoric, defined here as the study of writing or speaking as a means of communication, can provide the tools students need today to become savvy, responsible digital consumers. It is not a new role for rhetoric, but as the field of journalism morphs and technology proliferates, it is an increasingly critical role.

Several phenomena are affecting what we see and hear today. First is the speed at which we are receiving and disseminating information due to ever faster hardware; the ubiquity of personal technology; and the multiplicity of forms of connection, especially social media. This speed affects everything from politics to the arts. A few years ago, through tweets, texts, and video, we were able to see events unfold in Tahrir Square, Egypt, as they happened. Half a world away, in real time, we saw a man gunned down and a journalist beaten. A few days later we saw people cheering and embracing as President Mubarek resigned. Much of what we saw came over smartphones from nontraditional media sources such as Twitter and YouTube. According to a 2015 Pew Research Center poll, "About 63% of Facebook and Twitter users say that they use those social media platforms as a major source for news about events and issues not involving friends and family." The poll also found that news-related use of social media was up 50% from two years before (Arlen).

Speed is also a significant factor in multiplying the power of word of mouth. The volume of tweets about a movie, for example, can help predict the opening weekend box office performance (Wasow et al.). A YouTube video can bring instant fame. In 2009, Susan Boyle, an unknown, middle-aged singer from a Scottish village became an overnight sensation around the world when her YouTube broadcast went viral. In a matter of two weeks in 2012, South Korean rapper PSY's "Gangnam Style" became the most-viewed video on YouTube, garnering 834 million viewers. The Facebook site of Grumpy Cat, started in 2012, had almost 9 million likes by 2016.

A second phenomenon is the hyping of news. TV networks competing with cable stations for viewers promote controversy and feed on disaster, streaming video 24/7. For instance, every scrap of news worthwhile or not about Jared Loughner, the Tucson shooter who gunned down six people in 2010, made its way to cable news. Reporters interviewed his high school math teacher. Television stations played a video he had made walking the halls of the community college. Hyping the news not only stirs controversy, but it promotes alarmism and can lead to less-than-reasoned responses, for example the U.S. invasion of Iraq following 9/11.

Media outlets also hype the news by hosting guests with diametrically opposed views just so they will argue about an issue. The stronger the disagreement the better, and if the guests don't argue, at least they can present opposing points of view. Giving equal time to both sides of an issue, for example the causes of climate change, with no objective analysis, leaves the audience with a distorted view of reality. This can have wide-reaching effects, for example, in the case of climate change, undercutting public support for environmental protections. This kind of debate also leads to dichotomous thinking that oversimplifies issues into two sides when in actuality there may be many points of view.

Journalists have traditionally served as middlemen, providing context for news in order to avoid oversimplification. They developed specialties and were responsible for making sure that information was presented ethically, that facts were checked, that sources were verified, that the whole picture was accurate and the coverage fair. The process of putting together a newspaper required creating a hierarchy for news and deciding who should be given a platform, usually someone with the credentials to speak about a subject: a title, a degree, experience. *Front Page*, the 2011 documentary about The New York Times, showed the newspaper's editor constantly challenging the reporter to make sure he had all the sources he needed to publish an article. Many newsrooms do not have the staff anymore to do this kind of careful checking.

A 2010 Pew Research Center's Project for Excellence in Journalism report surveyed newspaper executives and broadcasters. It found that:

> Among those who see values changing, there is a broad consensus about the direction—and it is primarily negative. When asked to explain what they mean, majorities of both groups appeared most worried about loosening standards (62% of newspaper executives and 67% among broadcasters), and the bulk of these responses referred to a decline in accuracy, a lessening of fact-checking, and more unsourced reporting. ("Survey of News Executives")

That was followed by, and closely linked to, an emphasis on speed, mostly in a negative light. "'I worry that journalistic standards are dropping in that blogging and celebrity gossip and Tweets are being confused with reporting and editing that passes a rigorous standard,' wrote one broadcast executive" ("Survey of News Executives"). Ed Wasserman, Washington and Lee Knight Professor of Journalism, referring to a "journalism of haste," said, "Much of the problem seems to derive from enshrining speed as an operational priority. Newspaper staffs accustomed to meeting end-of-day deadlines are now running on round-the-clock Internet time, as if that were essential to their authority. Is it really?" In trying to scoop their competitors, CNN, Fox, the Associated Press, and the Boston Herald all reported inaccurately in April 2013 that an arrest had been made in the Boston bombing long before one had (Rieder). Errors due to over-eager reporting are all too common these days.

The Rupert Murdoch scandal that began unfolding in 2011 corroborated the Pew report's findings. Not only was there a loosening of standards in his British tabloid News of the World, but there was clear violation of the law: bribery, illegal wiretapping, theft. The culture of the paper was to get information in whatever way possible, and the more it fed the public salacious, titillating details, the more the public's appetite for this kind of reporting grew. Sadly, observers agreed that Murdoch's paper was far from the only one acquiring information by unethical or illegal means.

Not only is journalism failing to provide quality control in many cases, but technology is making it easier for any Tom, Dick or Harry, regardless of credibility, to get a message out to a huge number of people. For example, Terry Jones, a pastor of a 50-member church in Florida, could threaten to burn the Koran and have his message go out across the internet, causing international consternation. In the past, he might have gotten a mention in his local paper as an eccentric crank. In 2011, Anders Brievik was able to post his 1500-page manifesto online for all the world to see before beginning his killing spree in Norway. Easier access to information certainly has its positive side also, and no one would suggest censoring the internet, but ease of access requires more sophistication, more critical awareness, on the part of the end receiver.

A third factor in the way that we receive information is our ability to personalize our news. With so many sources available, we don't ever have to hear an opinion different from our own. As the Pew study shows, many Americans are ensuring just that:

> Just 12% of Republicans describe themselves as regular CNN viewers, and for MSNBC, with its lineup of liberal hosts, the figure is 6%. Back in 2002, the study says, Republicans were as likely to watch CNN (28%) as Fox News (25%). On the flip side, Democrats make up 21% of the Fox audience, 47% of CNN's and 53% of MSNBC's. (Kurtz)

Why does this matter? Because democracy depends on a free and open exchange of ideas, and a willingness to compromise. Hearing only one side, never having one's views challenged, hardens listeners against other views. The son of a friend, for example, is a staunch conservative who listens to Rush Limbaugh through his headphones all day at his job but insists this practice does not affect his judgment. Progressives are just as apt to listen only to progressive commentators. I believe this hardening of views is a strong factor in the gridlock that has made it so difficult for Congress to move forward in recent years.

Finally, the form in which the message reaches us shapes our perceptions. When people had to pick up a newspaper or watch the evening news to learn about world events, they were getting a fuller, more nuanced understanding than if they are scanning a Yahoo headline or a Twitter summary. These can give a person a false sense of being up on the news while he or she is only getting a boiled down, oversimplified version.

Children today are exposed to technology at a very early age. By the time they arrive at college, they are almost all technologically savvy, so we assume they know how to decode information. Not so, and having a college degree provides no guarantee either. Authors of the book *Academically Adrift* studied the increase in critical thinking and writing skills of 2300 students at 24 universities over the course of four years. More than a third showed no improvement. Fifty percent said they did not have a course in their previous semester that required a total of 20 pages of writing (Arum and Roksa). And we all know how many students read widely these days. The result is students with more access to information than ever before but less sophistication generally in interpreting it. This is crucial, not just in order to have an informed, responsible citizenship, but for the changing job market. In an editorial in the *New York Times*, Thomas Friedman said of today's leaner job market, "They are all looking for the same kind of people—people who not only have the critical thinking skills to do the value-adding jobs that technology can't, but also people who can invent, adapt and reinvent their jobs every day, in a market that changes faster than ever" (A27).

One of the most important skills in decoding information is simply being able to identify main ideas. This is essential to critical thinking. Without this ability to recognize the heart of a message, a person can unconsciously appropriate the opinions of others, be manipulated by them, or misinterpret messages. Further, without the ability to formulate an arguable thesis or establish a clear focus, students will produce writing that lacks unity and fails to persuade. Add in multimedia and digital composing and the process becomes even more complicated.

An expert on the Israeli/Palestinian conflict said recently that the first step in any peace agreement is being clear about what the two sides disagree about. What is the issue? This is not an easy question. Practice is necessary for students to learn how to tease out the point at issue. Anyone who doubts this can ask a room full of students the main point of a reading and see how many different answers come up. Simply assigning reading does not cut it, but teaching this kind of basic rhetorical skill is within reach of any instructor willing to slow down and analyze how and what an author is doing.

No one is going to turn the clock back on technology or journalism. In fact, the changing nature of journalism and exponential growth of technology provide an opportunity, a kairotic moment if you will, for rhetoric. They heighten its importance and add new urgency to our role as teachers. Our students should know how to research, write, and document a paper. They should understand the mechanics of writing. These are all important, but I would argue that one of the most significant things we can teach them today is how to judge, evaluate, and interpret the overload of information available to them on a daily, moment-to-moment basis.

How Not to Lose the Message: Three Basic Principles

The following very basic principles of rhetoric can be incorporated into a variety of courses, from freshman composition to media studies. I will discuss below the rationale for choosing each one and practical ways to incorporate them into the classroom:

- The connection between rhetoric and community
- The value of listening to and respecting multiple points of views
- The importance of questioning what we hear and read

The Connection Between Rhetoric and Community

Why does this matter? Because rhetoric only becomes relevant when students see themselves as part of something larger with responsibility to that something. After all, don't we find the roots of rhetoric in the ancient Greek assembly and citizens' desire to effect change? Students should understand that they are members of a variety of communities, that issues arise out of those communities, that language both connects and divides people, and that they can effect change through their words. They should also learn to recognize language that manipulates and inflames rather than informs. Some of the following exercises can help students begin to see their relationship to the community in new ways:

- Community mapping: take a walk through the downtown area; observe resources, green spaces, ethnic and racial make-up, and types of businesses; ask about local concerns; report results in visual form to class.
- Incorporate service learning in order to help students understand the community better. I have begun requiring 20 hours of community service in many of my classes, including first-year writing. Student engagement in the community has been linked to student success and continued engagement upon graduation (Astin 259–261).
- Assign community-based learning projects in which students write for nonprofits, government agencies, and businesses, i.e. brochures, letters, websites, etc.
- Assign students to sit in at an open city meeting and report on issues discussed.

The following exercises can help students understand how language effects change:

- Look at rhetoric as a tool or technology for positive change: letters to editor, online petitions, blogs, websites, and how the mode affects the message.
- Find examples of the breakdown of civil discourse: hate speech, negative campaigning, nasty comments.
- Write letters, editorials, and proposals that argue for a specific change at the local level.
- Look at whose message is privileged in the media and why.
- Have students choose an important issue that they believe is not being discussed enough, then do speed dating in which students discuss their issues with successive partners.
- Do research on an issue related to their community service or the local community, such as teen pregnancy or homelessness. This research could be used to produce a report for the agency or for a community-based research paper.

The Value of Listening to and Respecting Multiple Points of Views

We need to make sure students understand that issues are complex with more than pro and con positions, and that each issue has multiple stakeholders. Important issues need to be understood in their historical and social contexts and cannot be boiled down to a tweet or a Yahoo headline. Students need to be willing to leave their comfort zones to hear opinions that differ from their own. As UVA

Professor Mark Edmundson says in "Dwelling in Possibilities," "For a student to be educated, she has to face brilliant antagonists. She has to encounter thinkers who see the world in different terms than she does." The following exercises can help student identify a variety of positions and stakeholders for issues:

- Write an argument from one perspective, then write it from an alternative perspective. Neither should be pro or con.
- Do a case study in small groups. Each group chooses an issue currently in the news to investigate. They write a position paper as a group, then each person takes a different point of view from which to write an argument, for example 9/11 events have been omitted from many school curriculums because they are difficult to explain. Points of view could include a 9/11 survivor, a high school history teacher, and a first responder on 9/11.
- Assign liberal leaning students to listen to or read a media source that is generally considered conservative and conservative-leaning students one that is considered liberal. They should report on what issues were discussed and if they heard what they expected.
- Have students research a controversial issue. Have them discuss the issue in pairs where they practice dialogue—listening carefully and responding to one another's ideas.
- Choose a current issue. Compare reports from a variety of media sources: newspaper, blogs, Tweets, YouTube.

The Importance of Questioning What We Hear and Read, and the Value of Knowing What Questions to Ask

Our country cannot afford to have citizens who assimilate information uncritically, but critical thinking does not come naturally. It needs to be taught. Students need to know what questions to ask; for example, they should be asking the source of information and how current, unbiased and accurate the information is. They need to be able to identify fallacies in arguments. They should ask what information has been left out or misinterpreted, i.e. how ethical an argument is. Students do not need to be experts on the subject to ask critical questions of all claims and beliefs, including their own. The following list can give students an idea of the questions they can ask:

- What is the issue?
- What is the purpose?
- What appeals is the author using: ethos, pathos, logos?
- How does the choice of words affect the message?
- What are the assumptions behind the arguments?
- How current is the data? How credible are the sources?
- Could the statistics be interpreted differently?
- What significant information has been omitted?

- Does the medium affect the message? Compare the same information coming via different platforms: email, Tweets, text, blogs, etc.

Conclusion

The 2012 report from the National Task Force on Civic Learning and Democratic Engagement said that "Civic learning that includes knowledge, skills, values, and the capacity to work with others on civic and societal challenges can help increase the number of informed, thoughtful, and public-minded citizens. . . . Civic learning should prepare students with knowledge and for action in our communities."

As technology expands, media clutter will only increase. This is the one thing we can be sure of. There are many ways, however, no matter what we are teaching, to prepare students to be shrewd, critical consumers of information, to prepare them to not just be buffeted by the tides of the media, new and traditional, but when necessary to swim against the tide. The rhetorical concepts we teach, then, are an essential part of civic learning. They are tools students need to navigate in our media-saturated, digital age, surely a necessity for a responsible and engaged citizenship.

Works Cited

Arlen, Gary. "Pew: Social Media are Major Sources for News, Current Events." *The Business of Television Broadcasting and Cable*, vol. 14, July 2015.

Arum, Richard, and Josipa Roksa. *Academically Adrift: Limited Learning on College Campuses*. University of Chicago Press, 2011.

Astin, Alexander. "How Undergraduates are Affected by Service Participation." *Journal of College Student Development*, vol 39, no. 3, May/June 1998, pp. 259–261.

Crowley, Sharon, and Debra Hawhee. *Ancient Rhetorics for Contemporary Students*, 4th ed. Pearson Longman. 2009, p. 48.

Friedman, Thomas. "The Start-Up of You." *The New York Times*, 13 July 2011.

Giles, Martin. "Beyond the PC." *The Economist*, 8 October 2011, pp. 3–20.

Kurtz, Howard. "Multitasking Through the News." *Washington Post*, 12 September 2010.

National Task Force on Civic Learning and Democratic Engagement. Highlights from a Crucible Moment: College Learning and Democracy's Future, 10 January 2012.

Rieder, Rem. "On Boston Bombing, Bedia are Wrong—Again." *USA Today*, 19 April 2013.

Schmidt, Gregory. "Digital Technologies for Children." *The New York Times*, 10 December 2014.

"Survey of News Executives: News Leaders and the Future." Project for Excellence in Journalism, 2010.

Wasow, O., A. Baron, M. Gerra, K. Lauderdale, and H. Zhang. "Can Tweets Kill a Movie? An Empirical Evaluation of the Bruno Effect." Presented at the workshop on Microblogging at the Conference on Human-Computer Interaction (CHI), 11 April 2010.

Wasserman, Ed. "Looking Past the Rush Into Convergence." *Nieman Reports*, Winter 2006.

Chapter 3. Introductory Writing as the Gateway to Stronger Communities, College and Career Success

Karen Bishop Morris

PURDUE UNIVERSITY CALUMET

This chapter speaks to the powerful role writing can play in retaining students and maximizing their capacity to bridge significant gaps in pre-college preparation while laying the foundation for their future civic and professional participation. I will also raise issues for programs to consider when making the decision to integrate experiential learning (or *ExL*) into first-year composition classes. Finally, I end with a call to action to consider community-based writing as a vital outcome in first-year composition.

Zlotkowski in "Linking Service-Learning and the Academy: A New Voice at the Table?" argues that unless service-learning advocates become far more comfortable seeing enhanced learning as the horse pulling the cart of moral and civic values, and not vice versa, service learning will continue to remain less visible and less important to the higher education community as a whole than is good for its own survival. I am arguing for a shift in that perspective. Today's "reoccurring doomsday headlines citing poor graduation rates and decreasing literacy among [high school and college] students" beg for a different metaphor. The problem with the horse and buggy metaphor is that it privileges academic discourse over moral and civic values. If we consider that many of our students, in particular the first-generation ones that I have sought to use service-learning approaches to teach writing to, the success of the methodology lies in the very fact that these students identify more closely with the civic and moral aspects of their lives; the academic zone is often completely new territory. The truth: we haven't been very successful pulling them along anywhere; moral and civic values aren't just along for the ride. We must engage students at the intersection of their authentic interests and values. Moral and civic values are not mere accompaniments to learning but rather the gateway to the social and economic networks that often elude our first-generation populations. ExL can be the means by which students acquire the cultural capital necessary to navigate their journey through the academic world as they make relevant connections to external communities. Writing, then, becomes the catalyst, the raw power that multiplies and intensifies students' abilities to make connections to their extant belief system and to reflect in meaningful ways. It is no longer enough to orient students to academic prose in first-year writing when we so clearly have the power to transform them by giving them the access to a vision for the rest of their lives

. . . a vision that begins, not ends, with exploring the moral and civic obligations they already readily identify with.

Case in point: Esperanza Dillon. Esperanza was an above-average, non-traditional student who landed in my comp course ten years ago. Around week seven I decided to recap the research process and prepared to frame the final "big" research paper for the course. The more I talked, the more I could not ignore that sinking feeling that accompanies slow recognition. I had lost these folks. I cut the lecture and opted instead to pull up a chair in the center of the circle. "Ok, so tell me, what's on your mind? What are you thinking?"

Esperanza broke the silence, her voice shaky at first but getting stronger as she proceeded: "Dr. B, I don't want to speak for anyone else in this class. I think you're really a good teacher and I know you're telling us the things we need to know, but I'm overwhelmed. I'm a single parent and I graduate in December. I don't have a job and from the looks of this research you want us to do, I'll never find one 'cuz I'll be stuck in the library." I asked Esperanza and the others to think about this for a moment and then write down any ideas they had about ways to make this research assignment applicable to Esperanza's job search. Blank stares. Blank pages. "I'm sorry," she piped up again. Her voice broke, tears followed. "I'm just afraid I'm running out of time—out of options."

I knew I could help Esperanza navigate this assignment and discover some of the things she needed to know about herself and the workplace; however, I wasn't clear about how to do it in a way that would be meaningful to everyone else in the room—many of them two or three years away from graduation and lacking the urgency surrounding her specific circumstances. I decided in that moment that as long as students were engaged in genuine inquiry, there was no way this work— yet to be defined—could fail. Esperanza's inquiry was a job search, so my next question and her response triggered a paradigm shift in my approach to training others to teach freshman composition: "Esperanza, if you could wave a wand and have any job in the world today, what would it be?" To which she replied, "Oh, that's easy. I want to work at the Wrightsville Literacy Center—a paying position. I volunteer their now, but even that's gonna come to an end soon because we lost our funding." To which I replied, "Now we're getting somewhere! Your project, simply defined, is to plan a research project that investigates funding opportunities and benchmarks Wrightsville against other literacy centers—regionally and nationally. The deliverable: we write a grant. Best case: grant gets funded, you get your wish. Worst case: you learn new skills and find a job as a grant writer." And to the class: "Everyone, follow Esperanza's lead and write for fifteen minutes about a campus or community group you're either connected to or have some interest in. Brainstorm. What do you think is researchable about this organization and make guesses about possible writing projects that could be helpful to their mission or goals?" There was one other event that made Esperanza's plea hit a new nerve and made me commit to teaching community-based writing in composition classes from that day forward: just a few weeks prior our class sat in silence as we watched, together, the second plane crash into the Twin Towers. The gravity of 9/11 coupled with the urgency of Esperanza's job search brought several issues into sharp relief. I started thinking about how our students measure their success, how our culture measures the success of our students, and finally, what could be accomplished in the writing classroom to reconcile all of this with what the field of composition studies has defined as desirable outcomes. What I heard in class that day was an expressed disconnect between what students were expected to learn and what students were expected to be able to *do* with what they learn.

Pierre Bourdieu in 1986 raised the question of cultural capital and its application to discussions of aptitude and academic success. Historically disadvantaged youth in today's academic settings exhibit the same gap in measures tracking their success as did the students identified by Bourdieu nearly thirty years ago. At that time, Bourdieu criticized human capital theorists for taking into account only the economic investments made into educational activity. The prevailing attitude then was to focus on measuring actual dollars spent or even time spent studying as a quantifiable indicator of student achievement. There was absolutely no serious thought given to the link between economic capital and cultural capital transmitted to different levels of society (48). In his discussion of cultural capital, Bourdieu goes to great lengths to illuminate distinctions between cultural and economic capital; he describes the net effects or profits gained when either type of capital is transmitted and ultimately reproduced in society. There are two aspects of Bourdieu's theory of cultural capital that undergird my claim about the value of ExL as the irrefutable gateway for first-year (and first-generation) college students. The first is his recognition of cultural capital as *the work of acquisition*; the second is its rather hidden or invisible nature. The acquisition aspect suggests that gains in cultural capital are the result of work over time—not a specific time period, but enough time to reflect the relevant knowledge and values of a particular social class or situation. In other words, cultural capital cannot be transmitted instantly but rather it is accumulated in ways that define its success in terms of assimilation and even mastery. If we accept this explanation, then there is real value in exposing students to situations in which they can begin to sow the seeds necessary to acquire cultural capital early on. The invisible or hidden transmission of acquisition is also apparent when we speak about first-year composition students. In our composition classrooms, we are always striving to transmit and reproduce a level of competency in the structure of our assignments, our style of response to student essays, and so on. It is often not until our students have some breakthrough in the process—an aha! moment—that we can really be sure that they have acquired the capital of written literacy. The speed with which this acquisition happens, Bourdieu tells us, is also linked to the initial accumulation and transmission of cultural capital from the outset, or let's say from parents or the immediate home environment to students or their children. Children from families "endowed with strong cultural capital" and exposed at an early age will assimilate faster (49). This brings us to a third type of capital requisite for student success—social capital—which Bourdieu defines thusly:

> Social capital is the aggregate of the actual or potential resources which are linked to possession of a durable network of more or less institutionalized relationships of mutual acquaintance and recognition—or in other words, to membership in a group— which provides each of its members with the backing of the collectivity-owned capital, a 'credential' which entitles them to credit, in the various senses of the word (51).

Bourdieu's theory of forms of capital presents a unique opportunity for writing programs around the issue of engagement, and quite possibly insight into what ails public education in America.

I am in good company when it comes to pondering ways to address deficiencies in first-year students and seeing the transformative power of ExL as a pathway to student engagement. The statistics at my regional campus are alarmingly consistent with the national statistics on the effects of student engagement on the success of first-year college students. Paradoxically, now more than ever, even though there seem to be greater numbers of students—especially those from historically underserved populations—entering college, there are staggeringly fewer who seem to finish. George Kuh and his colleagues reported recently in *The Journal of Higher Education* that "Only half (51%) of students who enrolled at four-year institutions in 1995–96 completed bachelor's degrees within six years at the institutions at which they started." The figures are even more dismal for those who transferred and attended two or more institutions prior to obtaining baccalaureate degrees (540). If students are leaving early, then they are leaving with little or no opportunity to acquire cultural or social capital, which begs the question: *If we seize the opportunity of first-year writing to expose students to social networks and teach them how to navigate cultural contexts, might they stay?*

The external pressures placed on higher education experience regarding completion and graduation rates are very present, very real: "Students leave college for a mix of individual and institutional reasons: change of major, lack of money, family demands, and poor psycho-social fit, among others" (Kuh, Cruce, Shoup, and Kinzie 541). In fact, there have been numerous studies which take up each of these economic and social reasons, individually and in relation to one another which have yielded solid information for educators to propose interventions in the first and second year college experience. And even though we recognize these individual factors and persist in our interventions, something gets lost in the translation when we try to universalize our approach to addressing student engagement. Take Braxton's 2006 *National Postsecondary Education Cooperative* study that concluded there are "eight domains of student success that warrant attention" and specifies preparation for adulthood and citizenship, personal accomplishments, and personal development, as three of those domains.

One year later, a literature review sponsored by the same organization and this time led by George Kuh restated these areas in a broader fashion, for example, "engagement in educationally purposeful activities" and "acquisition of desired knowledge, skills and competencies." While this later language may move us closer to measuring educational outcomes, I cannot help but think about what we lose when we erase the language pointing to *personal* development, *personal* accomplishment *and* preparation for *citizenship*. The importance of those attributes is minimized if not fully effaced.

The questions guiding Kuh's later study sought to determine the impact of engagement on student success in the first year of college and net effects of pre-college achievement and experiences. The later study aimed to determine whether the effects of that engagement were general or conditional, in other words, widely observed or specific to some condition like gender or strength of pre-college preparation. Kuh's study is an elegant account of social, economic, and cultural factors that embody two significant takeaways for those of us engaged in teaching composition in the freshman year. The first finding states "student engagement in educationally purposeful activities is positively related to academic outcomes as represented by first-year student grades and by persistence between the first and second year of college." The really interesting news behind this finding is that while pre-college experiences (read: preparation) matter where first-year grades are concerned, once there has been a meaningful first-year experience the net effect of pre-college preparation "diminishes considerably." The second finding states that "engagement has a compensatory effect on first-year grades and persistence to the second year of college at the same institution. We are more likely to retain students, in other words, regardless of their backgrounds and risk factors, if they have been involved in developing cultural capital and thus participating in social networks on campus" (Kuh et al., 555).

Some clarification is necessary here regarding the usage of the phrase *student engagement*. The discourse of education tends to identify activities designed to enrich student engagement such as first-year experience courses or supplemental instruction. The kind of engagement I am advocating is immersion in real-world writing situations that require students to research, write, and think beyond the boundaries of a textbook or classroom space; the kind of engagement that allows students to acquire cultural and social capital while meeting the demands of their subject matter assignments; the kind of engagement that blurs the lines between their college experience and their personal life and puts them immediately on a pathway to student success. Studies conducted by BCSSE and NSSE show a sharp contrast in what faculty members and institutions provide in the way of academic and non-academic experiences and the significantly higher expectations of students. On almost every data point—rigor of academics, opportunities for social interaction with faculty and students, and so on—what participating institutions delivered fell far short of student expectations. On the other hand, when a pilot group in that same survey was isolated to participate in customized learning activities that were collaborative, provided social opportunities with diverse students and faculty, and upped the ante on academics, students reported significant gains in their experience of the first year of college (NSSE 2011).

Thoughts on Course Design

Esperanza worked diligently over an eight-week period interviewing board members, situating her knowledge of literacy centers, soliciting letters of support from the community and complaining less and less about the workload. Because of her outside responsibilities and childcare challenges, I became her *de facto* teammate. I shared my own samples of grants written over a ten-year period, and helped her after hours and on weekends in coffee shops to craft language appropriate for a panel of blind reviewers. Others in the class worked in teams of two or three and, while their projects were slightly less ambitious, their enthusiasm was just as fervent. Perhaps the biggest decision regarding course design that has carried over from the initial experience is that the experiential projects are not an optional assignment in the course; everyone must participate with a partner or in a team of three. The second characteristic is that at least one student in the team must have an existing connection to the group or organization, or at least a genuine area of inquiry to drive their investigations with the community partner. Herein lies the answer to the biggest criticism I hear when I speak to colleagues about wide-scale application of ExL in composition classes. They say it can't be done because of the sheer numbers of students filtering through our programs (3800 each academic year in my case); there aren't enough organizations to tap into, exclaim the naysayers. The bigger part of that issue is, and I agree, managing so many community relationships in a responsible, ethical way. I am not saying our system is without flaws, but I am saying that waiting until we have it all figured out is not the solution. On the first point about having enough project sites, in three years of adopting this experiential approach in our second semester course we have never even come close to being at a loss for project sites. Some students take the obvious routes of partnering with local non-profits. Charities are chosen because someone on the team has a personal connection—a loved one has been diagnosed or lost to a disease. Others research, write and offer recommendations to campus units like the Honors Program (again, typically someone in the group is a member) or tackle more widespread campus issues like the parking problem. The key lies in the authentic connection. It is essential for students to find value in a group they already belong to; it is way we begin to seed their personal power. If students can redefine their existing affiliations through the lens of academic discourse, then we accelerate the process of them building cultural capital.

Sometimes a class will identify a theme, like nutrition, and all of the projects in that class will investigate some aspect of nutrition. In a recent example, one group in a class working collaboratively on nutrition had a nursing student in the group and developed a webzine and social media accounts to share information with students about making healthy eating choices. A group in that same class wrote a children's book targeting childhood obesity and developed a fictional character, Riley the Rabbit, who was in a race to making better choices in the face of a world of temptations. That particular group conducted an online interview with an administrator at a pediatric clinic several states away as well as a third grade elementary teacher at a rural school that had recently been in the news for their innovative approaches to dealing with childhood obesity. To date, both the pediatric clinic and the third grade class have purchased sets of Riley's Race for a fall 2012 adoption.

These ExL projects are not all fun and games; the student teams usually encounter serious frustration defining their projects and establishing a workable project plan. I also remind instructors teaching the course to warn students that things will fall apart: their community contact will go AWOL; their group members will not post the meeting notes to the wiki in a timely fashion—or ever; the direction of their project will shift. In the next breath, I tell them that all of this adversity is unexpected but not unwelcome; the teachable moments abound in and through how well they are able to address challenges *in writing*. Students and instructors find comfort in knowing that their job is not to make whatever problems they encounter disappear, but rather explain the circumstances, regroup and adjust their plan and explain it—*in writing*.

It happened with Esperanza. We ran through three different contacts at the foundation and endless red tape securing approval from the soon-to-be defunct literacy center board to grant permission to make application for the funds. There wasn't enough time to research sufficiently and write the narrative, but we submitted the grant in spite of ourselves and miracles do happen: the request—two years' salary support for an Executive Director—was approved. Esperanza was the new face of literacy in Wrightsville; it was a watershed moment that changed my teaching forever. The following semester, I introduced the project day one so that students could take full advantage of having enough time to think through their group affiliations. As fate would have it, one of the students in class volunteered at the literacy center, and another student had visited the literacy center on a few occasions with a neighbor—a retired school teacher. These students were aware of Esperanza's recent hire, but they were not familiar with the details of the class project. A few weeks later, when asked to begin writing to explore their existing group memberships, these same two students expressed an interest in doing a project connected to the literacy center. The need: to create a training manual for community volunteers who represented various levels of education and various walks of life. There was a third generation of the Wrightsville Literacy project one year later when another group of students decided to develop a marketing plan to create awareness and visibility for the center on campus and throughout the community.

I want to be perfectly clear that I am not advocating for a reductionist and uncritical approach to ExL. There are significant issues concerning large-scale adoption and integration of ExL into composition programs. There is the ethical dilemma of managing a pipeline of students dispatched to engage with the larger community. Perhaps the question that haunts me most is *what are students getting out of what we are doing and how can I know for sure?* ExL should be more than just "a path from the classroom to the community." Rather we should be aiming for a materialist rhetoric that begins when we "use the laboratory of community-based writing projects in order to generate new questions for rhetorical theory, rhetorical practice, and rhetorical education" (Coogan 670).

Our first-year students are not ready to take up the task of transforming the field of rhetorical education, but I do know our students are quite capable of transforming themselves through civic and personal education. The idea of harnessing public power to evoke personal transformation has been written about by Higgins, Long, and Flower and they, too, acknowledge that we should be talking about transformation in relationship to it being one measure or outcome in assessment. In fact, they write very candidly about the observable confidence that student-rhetors develop as they find their voice and begin to realize that their community/audience stakeholders are invested and interested in what they bring to the table, in what they have *to say*:

For all the bravado displayed by teens in our projects, for all the self-confidence they exude in each other's company, they often fail to believe that adults can or will listen to them or even that they should. They, and many disenfranchised stakeholders we have worked with, often buy into dominant discourses that construct them as *the problem*, rather than people with potential to solve problems, and as incapable or untrustworthy rhetors with nothing worthwhile to contribute. At first tentative about their own ability to speak and be heard these stakeholders become more confident as they talk across the table, are acknowledge by others, and see their private memories and feelings celebrated in print. (192)

Conclusion

Responsible writing program administration means striking the right balance between helping students integrate their academic and personal lives and teaching them the strategies required to do so. Here are some strategies on programmatic, institutional, and national levels to help us move closer to the reality of integrating ExL into composition studies.

A first step should involve establishing parameters for community-based writing projects that the instructional staff feels confident and comfortable to implement. At PUC we have a cadre of instructors for whom our ExL research course hinges on print-based textual production that is decided upon in consultation with the community groups' needs. A second cadre of instructors embraces a multimodal approach to teaching; production for students in these sections requires podcasts, scripts, and webzines as evidence. Yet a third approach strongly recommended for those new to the program is writing *about* the community. These research projects are informed by field work (i.e. interviews and observations); however, they are less dependent on instructors and students producing texts in genres for which the conventions of same may be unfamiliar. Above all, programs should place a premium on teacher training to ensure best practices—academic and cultural—as well as ethical conduct and consistency in delivering instruction. While the goal is not and will never be to have every section duplicate the exact same experience, writing program administrators must be realistic about the fact that instructors will bring varying levels of workplace writing experience to these teaching situations and must fill in the gaps accordingly.

Writing programs must also recognize the impact of formalized assessment practices on ExL. Some possibilities include surveying students on their pre-college experiences and preparation, documenting the list of community partners students are working with, collecting and analyzing data regarding retention rates for students from the first to the second year, writing assessments that compare students' competence prior to take the freshman course with an experiential component and then again at later data points to determine the long-term impact of collaborative learning on student success. The best assessment designs will take into account the unique local characteristics embedded in the program and institutional context. All programs in the end will benefit from the legitimacy that comes as the result of engaging in sustained reflective practice.

Programs must work within their institutions to formalize partnerships with other academic units focused on student success: financial aid, centers for student achievement, placement offices/advising, and so on. It is important to ensure that community-based writing projects are being carried out in a way that is appropriate and consistent with the university's mission. In my case at PUC, ExL is a cornerstone of the campus's decadal plan as well as the overall strategic plan. If this kind of explicit support for experiential activities is not part of the institutional culture, then it is critical that the writing program administrator or instructional staff working with students find a way to plug-in to the mission with ExL as the preferred pathway. For instance, for campuses that have identified technology as a priority, designing a course that takes advantage of the full complement of multimodal affordances may be the way to go. If global education is a priority and ExL is not, then introducing students to more diverse community resources or other faculty with a different background may be the way to go.

Finally, in the spirit of the language that framed the WPA outcomes statement over ten years ago, I would like to see community-based writing assignments written into the statement to ensure that programs nationally are thinking about this as a pathway to student engagement and student success. In addition to the outcomes stated by the Council of Writing Program Administrators, here is what we have written into the outcomes for first-year writing at Purdue University Calumet:

Community-Based Writing

- Engage students in exploring their existing community connections and group memberships as potential sites for research and writing

- Practice modes of inquiry related to field work
- Analyze issues from a variety of theoretical lenses including cultural, historical, political, etc.
- Teach students what it means to situate knowledge in various contexts
- Collaborate with peers in making choices and producing texts using multimodal affordances
- Reflect on the experiential process
- Disseminate the experiential projects to a campus and/or community audience.

In many ways our work has only just begun when it comes to being able to offer up a complete model for assessing the range of community-based projects that occur in our writing classrooms. We have come very far in articulating our goals in terms that make sense for the university community and our outcomes in ways that help instructors and students grasp the connection between what we are teaching, what they should be learning, and how it will be useful immediately in their personal and professional lives. At PUC like at so many campuses, we recognize the value of being proactive where assessment is concerned. The difference here is where we choose to start the conversation. We are not putting the cart before the horse, but we are showing students the contents of the cart and encouraging them to remove those items most familiar and most interesting to them to share the saddle as they ride off into the sunset of the most important years of their lives.

Works Cited

Bourdieu, Pierre. "The Forms of Capital." *Handbook of Theory and Research for the Sociology of Education*, edited by J.G. Richardson. Greenwood Press, 1996, pp. 241–258.

Coogan, David. "Service Learning and Social Change: The Case for Materialist Rhetoric." *College Composition and Communication*, vol. 57, no. 4, 2006, pp. 667–693.

Higgins, Lorraine, Elenore Long, and Linda Flower. "Community Literacy: A Rhetorical Model for Personal and Public Inquiry." *Writing and Community Engagement: A Critical Sourcebook*, edited by Thomas Deans et al. Bedford/St. Martin's, 2010.

Kuh, George D. "Analysis: What Student Engagement Data Tell Us about College Readiness." *AACU*, vol. 1, no. 9, 2007, pp. 4–8.

Kuh, George D., Ty M. Cruce, Rick Shoup, and Jillian Kinzie. "Student Learning Outside the Classroom: Unmasking the Effects of Student Engagement on First-Year College Grades and Persistence." *The Journal of Higher Education*, vol. 79, no. 5, 2008, pp. 540–563.

National Survey of Student Engagement. "Fostering Student Engagement Campus-Wide—Annual Results 2011." Indiana University Center for Postsecondary Research, 2011.

Zlotkowski, Edward. "Linking Service-Learning and the Academy: A New Voice at the Table?" *Change*, vol. 28, no. 1, 1996, pp. 20–27.

Chapter 4. The Value of
Violence in Student Writing

Lori D. Brown
ASSOCIATION FOR SUPERVISION AND CURRICULUM DEVELOPMENT

Columbine. Virginia Tech. School names forever associated with deadly, senseless acts of violence committed by their own students. But the shootings are linked by more than guns, grief, and shattered communities. In both massacres, the shooters prefaced their in-school carnage with violent writings that alarmed English/ Creative Writing instructors.

Two months before the April 20, 1999, shooting, Columbine shooter Dylan Klebold wrote a dark short story for his Creative Writing class with English teacher Judy Kelly. The story described a black, trench-coat clad shooter with pistols in a backpack (Cullen; Hudson, *Student*; Langman, Lieberman). Kelly explained that Klebold's text was "the most vicious story I have ever read" (Lieberman 95). Similarly, shooter Seung Hui-Cho's texts of rape and murder troubled Virginia Tech classmates and professors so deeply that he was required to exit the formal English classroom setting and continue English studies in one-on-one tutoring provided by Department chair Lucinda Roy (Roy).

In both settings, the shootings were foreshadowed by a series of violence indicators, including disturbing written course assignments that forced the English / Creative Writing instructor into the role of *First Responder*. The term *first responder* is used in this context to explain that the academic instructor was among the first individuals within the school/university setting to encounter and grapple with the perpetrator's violent texts.

As the media became more aware of the violent and alarming nature of Cho's former writings and the fact that Dr. Lucinda Roy had tried for two years to warn the university that something that might happen, the media frenzy continued to intensify. Roy explains that every outlet from ABC and NBC to CNN, the BBC, Sky News (United Kingdom) and Japanese and Korean journalists descended on the Blacksburg campus to learn more about the tragedy and the events that prefaced the shooting.

This sort of mass media frenzy, which seems to be repeated any time there is a significant national shooting or violent act, evidences Sarah Hardison O'Connor's description, in this collection, of media *hyping*, meaning news and information is collected and disseminated so quickly so that the value and quality of the information is called into question. While O'Connor accurately explains that this sort of media hype has negative ramifications for student understanding of text and the accuracy and quality of written text, it can also be argued that this sort of media hype has a highly negative influence on educators, as it establishes an irrational fear that any student who writes of disturbing or violent themes has already designed and prepared to commit the next school massacre.

When irrational and unfounded fears emerge, the ability of instructors to accurately and with clarity assess and respond to student writing, particularly writing with violent themes or drawings, diminishes. Diminished capacity to carefully, patiently, and accurately review and respond to any sort of student text, fails to keep an instructor *neutral*, which according to Ruth Goldfine and Deborah Mixson-Brookshire in this collection is important if students are to interact effectively around and form their own opinions about controversial issues and or topics.

Although remaining neutral and open-minded about student selected topics/themes of interest, regardless of the amount of violence presented by such topics, is a key component of fair and equitable learning environments and composition classrooms, the fact remains that too many episodes of violent texts that prefaced violent events, and the accompanying media frenzy around those examples, just make violent writing instructor responses challenging and perhaps different from any other sort of student response. A brief overview of tragedies prefaced by violent student texts follows.

School Based Violent Texts from Violent Perpetrators

Many schools, including secondary and post-secondary institutions, have faced pre-shooting patterns of violent written expressions from the student perpetrators. These episodes often placed instructors/administrators into first responder roles. Examples include:

- Thurston High School in Springfield, Oregon, 1998—shooter Kip Kinkel wrote a school essay about love in which he indicated that only firearms could help him fight his unloved "cold, black heart" (Lieberman 95).
- East Carter High School in Grayson, Kentucky, 1993—shooter Scott Pennington kills his seventh-period English teacher, Deanna McDavid, claiming it was McDavid's continued questioning about his morbid writing that triggered the shooting (Lieberman).
- Frontier Junior High School in Moses Lake, Washington, 1996—shooter Barry Loukaitis wrote ninth-grade poems of a violent nature, including one entitled "Murder" (Fast 33). He committed the school shooting in February of his freshman year, at the age of 14.
- University of Iowa, November 1, 1991—Former Graduate Student Gang Lu (age 28) shot and killed 4 faculty members, 1 student, and injured others because of anger about the university overlooking him for a coveted dissertation prize. Lu's pre-shooting letters of complaint to university officials were never addressed (Marriott).

In addition to these examples of violent, school-based texts from violent perpetrators, we also know that some violent perpetrators wrote about and/or praised prior violent acts. Roy explains that shooter Cho wrote an eighth-grade text in which he described a desire to repeat the Columbine High School shooting. In this case, it is fair to say that Cho's teachers and educational community saw warning signs more than five years before his rampage. With each violent writing, Cho was expressing the thoughts of someone who was mentally stable and faced significant demons.

But the fact that Cho wrote of violent desires before committing his tragic violent act is very common, according to threat and risk assessment experts. In fact, the FBI refers to this phenomenon as *leakage*. Contrary to popular belief and media hype, violent perpetrators never snap, but rather build toward a violent act by intentionally or unintentionally leaking clues that reveal their disturbed state of mind and or harmful intentions. The FBI explains of this phenomenon:

> These [leaked] clues can take the form of subtle threats, boasts, innuendos, predictions, or ultimatums. They may be spoken or conveyed in stories, diary entries, essays, poems, letters, songs, drawings, doodles, tattoos, or videos. . . . Leakage can be a cry for help, a sign of inner conflict, or boasts that may look empty but actually express a serious threat. Leakage is considered to be one of the most important clues that may precede an adolescent's violent act. (O'Toole 16)

Although government research continues to confirm that schools are the safest places for youth to be (Fast), the media's intense coverage of school or university shootings, combined with indicators that violent shooters may precede their actions with violent writings, brings into question the *appropriate* role of violent writing in academic settings.

The prior massacres at Columbine and Virginia Tech, along with FBI documented evidence of leaked violent clues, force us to ask what to do with and how to respond to student created violent texts. After all, if a student writes of murder, rape, or suicide, then doesn't the phenomenon of leakage prove that he or she is actually leaking a real-world desire to engage in the described behavior? Furthermore, does this writing genre additionally require censorship, excessive disciplinary responses, or potentially an immediate expulsion and arrest for communicating a threat?

Perhaps surprisingly, the answer to these question is an emphatic *no*. Threat assessors, including Mohandie and the FBI (O'Toole) explain that most students who write violently are expressing their freedom to write creatively, and pose no threat to the academic environment. In fact, educational research provides evidence that K-16 students often write violently, but without subsequent violent acts. Examples follow.

K-16 Examples of Violent Writing

Educational research offers proof that students sometimes opt to write of violent themes. Teachers have reported encounters with violent themes ranging from suicide to sexual abuse, and in both personal and fictionalized student texts. Similarly, K-12 instructors encounter violent themes from students. Research finds prior documented encounters with violent texts among the following sub-populations:

- Boy writers (Fletcher)
- Gang-affiliated youth (Ma'ayan; Mahiri and Sablo; Moje)
- Urban, high-poverty minority youth (Ma'ayan; Weinstein)
- Adolescents from violent-laden communities (Mahiri and Sablo)

Encountered violent topics have included everything from Halloween-type horror stories and alien abductions (Fletcher) to gangsta prayers and parody poems containing descriptions of guns, bullets, or killings (Camitta; Moje). Brown additionally confirmed that high school English teachers report violent texts from ninth- to twelfth-grade students, including both males and females and from academically gifted and struggling students.

In addition to information about secondary students producing violent texts, Brown's study specifically considered instructor response. Data revealed that teachers may select a number of responses to violent texts, although some indicated in short-responses that they are unprepared to address or respond to violent texts. Instructor discomfort with response highlights the potential cause of school inaction or over-reaction to violent texts; school staff quite simply do not know how to address violent texts. Details about prior recorded responses follow.

Response to Violent Writing

O'Connor, in this volume, writes:

> Our country cannot afford to have citizens who assimilate information uncritically, but critical thinking does not come naturally. It needs to be taught. Students need to know what questions to ask; for example, they should be asking the source of information and how current the information is. (14)

In similar fashion, instructors confronted with response to student created violent texts must be able to similarly assimilate information critically, ask the right questions, and identify the source and accuracy of the provided text in question. In other words, instructors must be as critical as their students, with an open mind and comprehensive approach to any new text. But as evidence shows, sometimes the violent or disturbing nature of highly personal student themes makes response a challenging activity at best.

The K-12 Response

Teachers at the K-12 level, in similar fashion to peers in the post-secondary world, have many response options with violent or disturbing texts. Quantitatively documented K-12 responses to violent student texts have included the following:

- Discuss text with student (Brown)
- Discuss text with a counselor or other mental health professional (Brown)
- Discuss text with school-based administrator (Brown)
- Discuss text with other teachers or parents of student (Brown)
- Grade written text as normal (Brown)
- Censorship of text (Fletcher)
- Disciplinary or legal action, including school expulsions, suspensions, and jail time (Hudson Student Hudson, Silencing)

This list shows that responses fall along a broad spectrum of intensity, as dialoging with a student about his/her submitted violent text is quite a different response from a school-initiated expulsion or law enforcement pursued arrest followed by jail time. In fact, the extreme nature of turning to school suspensions and arrests for violent themes was on recent display in the media's coverage of a Summerville, South Carolina, high school student who was arrested and suspended for written text about killing his neighbor's pet dinosaur with a gun (Rivera and Jain). In this particular case it appears that the school failed to obtain the full context of the written text before resorting to the most extreme response possible.

The Post-Secondary Response

Although the Virginia Tech tragedy provides evidence of post-secondary responses to violent texts when connected with a student's rare and rather unusual silent behavior, many post-secondary responses to violent student texts have been considered within the broader context of "personal writings" (Connors), and particularly around personal writings of a self-disclosing nature. As Berman explains, self-disclosing personal writings revolving around somewhat intense themes may create instructor discomfort.

Instructors may censor or criticize personal, self-revealing student writings because they are academically inappropriate (Berman; Banks), or narcissistic (Bartholomae). Although Bartholomae never addresses the matter of violent or disturbing themes, he goes so far as to explain that any sort of student fostered personal writing is devoid of academic value for the formal classroom settings.

In contrast, some post-secondary instructors (Berman) encourage and embrace the personal, self-disclosing voice, even when intertwined with violent themes, for the role that it plays in student growth and development. Roy even argues that despite the Virginia Tech tragedy of 2007 and its explicit connection to violent texts, the violent student voice should not be silenced or censored, as we risk losing the sense of dialog among student peers and educators that is critical to growth and the advancement of knowledge. Additionally, excessive editing and censorship of student texts that make an instructor uncomfortable, particularly in the early years of one's schooling adventure, can "paralyze a young writer" (Roy 197) and even present mixed messages to students (as they often hear and read violent expressions in every day communications and among peers in local neighborhoods, social settings, and mass media).

It has even been argued that to deny a student of self-selected, personal writing themes is to deny personal identity (Blitz and Hurlbert). Additionally, censorship of the personal, violent voice may be seen as a rejection of the student's voice and culture; meaning their unsanctioned voices (Moje; Weinstein) are forced to yield to classroom accepted sanctioned voices devoid of personal, violent, or uncomfortable themes. In addition to concerns about censorship of student writing, this scenario begs the question of messaging to students. What sort of message does an instructor send to his/her students if the community-based voice is silenced the moment they step into a formal academic environment? The issue of sanctioned vs. unsanctioned classroom based literacies begets additional concerns around equitable learning for the advantaged and disadvantaged.

The Result of the Response

While opinions about the appropriateness or academic quality/validity of personal, self-disclosing writings may vary, educational institutions across the K-16 spectrum must acknowledge that violent writing should never be equated with intent to commit a real-world act of violence, *unless* identified as such by a highly trained threat and risk assessment team. In other words, institutions should never allow descriptions of the death of pet dinosaurs or a research paper on serial killings to lead to the conclusion that any student needs to be immediately suspended, expelled, arrested or even charged with communicating a real world threat.

To prevent inaccurate and extreme assumptions about student writer intent, educational institutions must adopt effective threat assessment processes that are openly known, communicated, enforced and practiced. Effective threat assessment procedures ensure a balanced approach to violent or disturbing writings, which is an absolute necessity if we adopt the notion that violent writing can at times serve a highly beneficial role for the student writer, including the opportunity to process the real world violence of his/her world.

Finding Value in the Violence

Research from three distinct fields of research (threat assessment, psychological, and educational) provides insight to the benefits of allowing students to write violently. The benefits include:

- Safety: Violent writing provides the disturbed/threatening students a forum for leaking clues, which triggers interventions to stop violent acts
- Health and Self-Advocacy: Violent writing is an outlet for healing from challenging and traumatic events, and a way to advocate for mental health support

- Educational: Violent writing is a forum for encouraging improved writing skills and breaking down barriers between sanctioned and unsanctioned literacies

Safety Benefits

Threat assessors and the law enforcement officials tasked with responding to violence welcome leaked, written clues that signal an individual is struggling with disturbed, violent, or threatening thoughts, as these clues may initiate a successful intervention process that stops a violent act and provides the writer with appropriate mental health support. In this regard, student created violent writing is both a clue and a calling: a calling for help. Langman explains that Columbine shooter Dylan Klebold's personal journals and papers were filled with repetitive clues of his dangerous and psychotic thoughts, but they went largely unnoticed by educators untrained to recognize text-embedded mental health clues.

Educators, particularly post-secondary educators who are often trained in their content field rather than in the broader field of educational practice, are never prepared to recognize written clues that indicate disturbed student thought, as that sort of training and activity is often reserved for those in the mental health and law enforcement fields of study. Consequently, placing blame on educators for failing to recognize a student's real world violent intent is frequently misplaced blame, as there is simply no way to provide all K-16 instructors with this form of highly specialized threat assessment training that studies written patterns, etc. But with that being said, it is important to note that institutions can take some steps to better prepare instructors for confronting and responding well to violent or disturbing student texts.

Although educators should never be asked to assume the role of threat assessor, they can be trained as first responders who recognize clues/warning signs or patterns of behaviors that merit further investigation by trained threat assessors. These threat assessors can in turn identify the types of clues that Langman explains may be presented in a potential perpetrator's written expression. As *first responders* instructors might be trained to simply recognize the following basic conditions:

- A student has a pattern of writing and/or speaking about violent and dark themes
- A written text details a fictionalized assault/attack within a setting or with characters who mirror real world characters and settings
- Student text is filled with a desire to engage in self harm (suicide, self-mutilation, etc.)
- Written texts convey an unusual obsession with violent weapons, acts, or figures
- A student's intense violent or disturbing writings seem to accompany a significant change in behavior

In each of these scenarios, an instructor is only being asked to be aware and to notice patterns of behavior or written expression. Awareness does not force a teacher into the inappropriate role of *threat assessor*, as that is not their role in the educational environment. But awareness can lead to the right persons who are capable of conducting effective threat and risk assessments, given what is known about the student's disturbing or frequent expressions. Once this information is transferred from teacher to threat and risk assessment team, the team can make a variety of decisions that may or may not include a comprehensive needs assessment process and that may even lead to getting the student appropriate mental health supports, if that is determined to be a need. When this happens, the teacher has taken the critical first step of letting others know that something may not be quite right, which allows other experts to play their role in the ongoing process of addressing student need.

The advantage of the establishment of sound threat and risk assessment procedures in educational settings is that the burden of action is removed from the shoulders of the instructor to a broader, more specialized group that has the background and knowledge to reach a more accurate conclusion surrounding student motives for violent texts. Thanks to the volume of post-Columbine threat and risk assessment research for school settings, institutions, particularly K-12 settings, have a myriad of school threat and risk assessment guidelines and recommendations for academic institutions from which to pull and implement (Fein et al.; O'Toole; Dwyer, Osher, and Warger; Mohandie; Cornell and Sheras). Today's schools have access to multiple free resources that help institutionalize comprehensive threat and risk assessment procedures that trigger accurate responses to violent writings or other potential threats.

At the post-secondary level, the errors of response at Virginia Tech have led to better resources for schools concerned with the balance between student privacy and mental health interventions, as part of the initial breakdown of communication around Cho's potential for violence revolved around prior ineffective mental health policies that led to a lack of shared information between the school, mental health specialists, and the student In fact, prior to the one year anniversary of the Virginia Tech shooting, Virginia Governor Kaine signed into law significantly revised mental health bills that would both reform and fund the state's struggling mental health services (Roy). If there is anything positive that emerged from the horrendous tragedies suffered at Virginia Tech and many other educational campuses between 1999 and 2007, it is the emergence of comprehensive models/resources for helping other schools address and try to prevent similar fates, many of which were newly designed with the direct assistance of our nation's top threat assessment experts and researchers.

In summary, academic institutions must embrace and train staff to understand the safety nets in place to keep all safe and secure, starting with classroom based responses to individual student cries for help through written violent or disturbing expression.

Health and Self-Advocacy Benefits

As previously stated, few students who write violently actually intend to commit violence. Instead, some students write violently as a way to process the violence they have encountered in their lives, communities, homes, and social settings. Similar to the aggressive student who writes of a violent incident in hopes that someone may notice his cry for help, a previously victimized student may write of a violent episode in hopes of obtaining some level of support to process the horror.

The victimized student who writes of a violent encounter with rape, bullying, or aggression may share these stories for the purpose of trying to determine why it happened and how to live with the assumed shame that may be associated with the violent act. In this context, psychological researchers would agree that a student's written description of the prior trauma is an effective way of beginning to process and heal.

Research shows that writing through our personal life challenges/traumas both develops the person (Berman) and heals the soul (DeSalvo). DeSalvo explains:

> The writing process, no matter how much time we devote to it, contains a tremendous potential for healing . . . writing about the traumatic events that we've experienced is an extremely helpful way of integrating them into our lives, of helping us feel happier, of improving our psychic and physical well-being (73, 159).

DeSalvo further explains that writing can be viewed as a necessary and significant act that synthesizes our thoughts, feelings, and experiences in a manner that promotes spiritual, emotional, and psychic wholeness.

Classroom based action research supports this finding, as Berman's survey of his graduate students revealed that 86% indicated that being allowed to write of personal, self-disclosing themes in the classroom contributed positively to their health, well-being, and emotional intelligence. In other words, students freely admit that being allowed to write of highly personal and self-disclosing themes is cathartic and useful. If that is the case, then any teacher's choice to censor these personal, self-disclosing topics (because they feel uncomfortable with the personal information) may prove more problematic than the initial writing itself.

Although the written texts of victims can be disturbing, graphic, or painful, broad scale censorship or avoidance of these written themes is in fact never advised. It is important for students to know that if they risk crying out for help, an adult on the receiving end of the written text is going to risk asking the student if he/she would like to speak with a trained professional who may help. Additionally, if the cry for help involves abuse for students under the age of 18, students need to know that schools will immediately make a referral to local DSS divisions. Because disturbing or violent texts hold the potential to both leak violent intentions and to provide a cathartic outlet for students faced with trauma, instructors should acknowledge that the silencing of either intent is potentially more harmful than beneficial, for both overall safety and personal well-being.

Educational Benefits

Writing begets better writing. We only improve as writers when we practice our written and spoken literacies in meaningful text activities. This basic premise of strong writing classrooms was highlighted by Applebee more than 30 years ago when he explained that in addition to being asked to write "more often" (99), students need to be engaged in meaningful written activities that require the production of new text and new meanings (in other words, limited multiple choice and fill in the blank activities across the disciplines, etc.). If English classrooms are bastions of intellectual freedom with equitable response to all student literacies, including those perhaps once viewed as unsanctioned or inappropriate for the classroom, then instructors must allow some creative license in the writing process.

In a study of adolescent girl literacies, including girls from high-poverty, violence-laden communities, Ma'ayan found that many adolescent girls failed to write of their violent communities and lifestyles because such themes were unwelcomed by instructors. When Ma'ayan allowed the girls outside opportunities to speak and write through their violent, crazy worlds, personal literacy improved, meaning students took a critical first step toward becoming improved literate citizens.

To teach students the value of intellectual freedom and to grow them as creative, powerful writers means we cannot shy away from uncomfortable themes. This includes avoiding censorship. Beyond the legal ramifications of censored student texts, censorship runs the greater risk of silencing the modern student voice and stunting literacy development. Even Roy argues the personal and violent voice still has a place in the classroom, even when it is unpredictable and uncomfortable.

But, it is important to note that while broad scale censorship of uncomfortable topics/themes is not recommended for the academic setting, "truly threatening speech is not constitutionally protected" (Oltman 26). In other words, freedom of creative expression does not mean that teachers should tolerate threatening expressions. Schools can take specific disciplinary steps to address threats, and they should address them swiftly. The challenge for teachers is determining whether violent or disturbing text is truly *threatening* or just weird. Because this challenge makes response to violent expressions difficult, the need for school and district leaders to support teachers with proper safe guards and strong threat assessment teams becomes even more critical when creativity proves challenging.

Proper Response to Violent Texts

As shown, violent writing is not necessary a bad phenomenon within the academic setting. When responded to properly, such texts can serve a beneficial role in the lives of student writers, including expanded creative thought, cathartic outlets, and improved written and literacy skills. But these benefits do not negate the fact that violent texts can also be leaked violent clues demanding a high higher level of broad-scale response, and for this reason, a balanced approach to these expressions is recommended.

The dual nature of violent expressions (resulting in both positive and negative outcomes) demands that schools and instructors take the time at the start of each new school year to carefully consider appropriate and sanctioned responses to violent texts. School leaders have no desire to see their staff plastered across the 6:00 p.m. news for arresting a young adolescent who wrote about killing a pet dinosaur. It does not help the school image and such extreme reactions can cause significant negative repercussions for students who actually communicated no known threat (long-term disciplinary reports that follow the student etc).

But on the other hand, school leaders have no desire to find themselves in the same situation as Virginia Tech with international stories about the way that the school avoided leaked clues from the deadly perpetrator. In fact, following many school shootings, schools, school boards, and educators have found themselves facing significant lawsuits for failure to address known leaked clues in advance of the tragedy.

To avoid either extreme, schools need to work closely with their instructors to determine a common language of response for student violent expressions. The response tips that follow provide a brief snapshot of potential actions leading to balanced educational responses. The tips can help successfully embrace, rather than censor or mishandle violent expressions. When these action steps are partnered with effective institutional threat and risk assessment procedures that are effectively communicated to call, good results will follow.

10 Instructor Tips

1. Acknowledge violent writing as a genre meriting the same consideration, and even expanded consideration, as other classroom genres
2. Realize that your own history, philosophies, thoughts and emotions may positively or negatively influence response
3. Realize that traditional educational assessments of violent texts may be an insufficient response
4. Avoid censorship because of personal discomfort, but recognize your freedom to identify limits of guidelines for written personal themes
5. Acknowledge the role of communication and speak safely with the violent writer
6. Know when to acknowledge your inability to properly respond and when to seek help from other professionals
7. Know your school's mental health policies and the institutional threat assessment process

8. Never assume a role beyond your expertise. You are not a threat assessor.
9. Share with students at the beginning of a course your anticipated approach or response to violent/disturbing texts, including your right to question, converse with other personnel, and/or contact guardians or institutional counselors (as appropriate and within FERPA or HIPAA guidelines)
10. Continuously revisit your anticipated responses to violent writing

Works Cited

Anderson, Charles M., and Marian M. MacCurdy. *Writing and Healing: Toward an Informed Practice*. National Council of Teachers of English, 2000.

Applebee, Arthur N., et al. *Writing in the Secondary School: English and the Content Areas*. National Council of Teachers of English, 1981.

Banks, William P. "Written through the Body: Disruptions and 'Personal' Writing." *College English*, vol. 66, no. 1, 2003, pp. 21–40.

Barron, Monica. "Creative Writing Class as Crucible." *Academe*, December 2007.

Bartholomae, David. "Writing with Teachers: A Conversation with Peter Elbow." *College Composition and Communication*, vol. 46, no. 1, 1995, pp. 62–71.

Berman, Jeffrey. *Diaries to an English Professor: Pain and Growth in the Classroom*. University of Massachusetts, 1994.

Berman, Jeffrey, and Patricia H. Wallace. *Cutting and the Pedagogy of Self-Disclosure*. University of Massachusetts Press, 2007.

Blitz, Michael, and Claude Hurlbert. *Letters for the Living: Teaching Writing in a Violent Age*. National Council of Teachers of English, May 1998.

Brown, L. "Violent Writing: A Quantitative Exploration of an Unexplored High School Phenomenon." Dissertation, Western Carolina University, 2011.

Camitta, Miriam. "Cross-cultural Approaches to Literacy." *Vernacular Writing: Varieties of Literacy among Philadelphia High School Students*, edited by Brian V. Street. Cambridge University Press, 1993, pp. 228–246.

Connors, R. J. "Personal Writing Assignments." *College Composition and Communication*, 1987, pp. 166–183.

Cornell, Dewey G., and Peter L. Sheras. *Guidelines for Responding to Student Threats of Violence*. Sopris West Educational Services, 2006.

Cullen, David. *Columbine*. Machete Book Group, 2009.

DeSalvo, Louise A. *Writing as a Way of Healing: How Telling Our Stories Transforms Our Lives*. HarperSanFrancisco, 1999.

Dwyer, Kevin P., et al. *Early Warning, Timely Response a Guide to Safe Schools*. U.S. Dept. of Educational Research and Improvement, Educational Resources Information Center, 1998.

Fast, Jonathan. *Ceremonial Violence: Understanding Columbine and Other School Rampage Shootings*. Overlook, 2009.

Fein, Robert A., et al. "Threat Assessment in Schools: A Guide to Managing Threatening Situations and to Creating Safe School Climates." U.S. Secret Service, 2002.

Fletcher, Ralph J. *Boy Writers: Reclaiming Their Voices*. Stenhouse, 2006.

Hudson, D. L., Jr. "Student Expression in the Age of Columbine: Securing Safety and Protecting First Amendment Rights." Rep. no., vol. 6, no. 2. The First Amendment Center First Reports, 2005.

———. The Silencing of Student Voices: Preserving Free Speech in America's Schools. First Amendment Center, 2003.

Hummel, M. "Crisis of Conscious: In the Aftermath of Virginia Tech, How Should Teachers Handle Disturbing Writing?" Poetry Foundation. www.poetryfoundation.org/article/180145?id=180145.

Hummel, M. "In the Aftermath of Virginia Tech, How Should Teachers Handle Disturbing Writing." Crisis of Conscious. Poetry Foundation.

Lankford, S. "Queers, Bums, and Magic: How Would You Grade a Gay-Bashing?" Presented at the Conference on College Composition, Washington, DC, 23 May 2003.

Langman, Peter F. Why Kids Kill: Inside the Minds of School Shooters. Palgrave Macmillan, 2009.

Lieberman, Joseph. School Shootings: What Every Parent and Educator Needs to Know to Protect Our Children. Kensington, 2008.

Ma'ayan, Hadar Dubowsky. Reading Girls: The Lives and Literacies of Adolescents. Teachers College, 2012.

MacCurdy, Marian M. "Writing and Healing: Toward an Informed Practice." From Trauma to Writing: A Theoretical Model for Practical Use, edited by Charles M. Anderson and Mariam M. MacCurdy. National Council of Teachers of English, 2000, pp. 158–200.

Mahiri, Jabari, and Soraya Sablo. "Writing for Their Lives: The Non-School Literacy of California's Urban African American Youth." The Journal of Negro Education, vol. 65, no. 2, 1996, pp. 164–80.

Marriott, M. "Iowa Gunman Was Torn by Academic Challenges." The New York Times, 4 November 1991.

Mohandie, Kris. School Violence Threat Management: A Practical Guide for Educators, Law Enforcement, and Mental Health Professionals. Specialized Training Services, 2002.

Moje, Elizabeth B. "'To Be Part of the Story': The Literacy Practices of Gangsta Adolescents." Teachers College Record, vol. 102, no. 3, 2000, pp. 652–690.

Morgan, Dan. "Ethical Issues Raised by Students' Personal Writing." College English, vol. 60, no. 3, 1998, pp. 318–325.

Oltman, Gretchen A. Violence in Student Writing: A School Administrator's Guide. Corwin, 2013.

O'Toole, Mary Ellen. The School Shooter: A Threat Assessment Perspective. FBI Academy, 2000.

Responding to Disturbing Creative Writing: A Guide for Faculty and GTAs [Policy]. Working paper. Virginia Tech, 2007.

Rivera, R., and S. Jain. "Police, Lawyer Release Statements on Student's Alleged Dinosaur Killing." WWBC NBC-12, 19 August 2014.

Roy, Lucinda. No Right to Remain Silent: The Tragedy at Virginia Tech. Harmony, 2009.

Valentineo, M.J. "Respond When a Life Depends on it: What to Write in the Margins when Students Self Disclose." Annual Meeting of the Conference on College Composition and Communication, Washington, DC, March 1995.

Weinstein, Susan. *Feel These Words: Writing in the Lives of Urban Youth*. State University of New York, 2009.

Chapter 5. Embracing Diversity in Composition Courses

Rachel McCoppin
University of Minnesota Crookston

The importance of diversity to a student's college experience is undisputed; countless universities discuss this importance in their mission statements, yet there is often confusion on how to incorporate diversity into the interdisciplinary curriculum and what the particular value of such coursework provides to students. Implementing classroom projects in writing courses that center on diversity is not always easy, but the value of multicultural experiences in college enables students to learn life-long lessons that will guide them in becoming better world citizens and will also aid their professional development. According to the Association of American Colleges and Universities (AACU) 2013 employer survey, "More than 9 out 10 of those surveyed say it is important that those they hire demonstrate ethical judgment and integrity; intercultural skills, and the capacity for continued new learning." The AACU defines a liberal education as providing the foundation for students to gain experience in practicing "ethical judgment and integrity" in intercultural situations. This chapter will therefore discuss opportunities for bridging intercultural experience with opportunities for ethical value judgment within composition courses in order to help students achieve applied intercultural skills needed for their various disciplines. First this chapter will explore occasions within the composition classroom where students can learn about their peers' background and openly discuss and write about cultural differences, as again the AACU points to a marked employer value of a student's ability to communicate across cultural boundaries. Furthermore, this chapter will offer suggestions to apply service learning opportunities to support composition assignments, as service learning provides not only applied real-world experience desired by many employers; "Employers strongly endorse educational practices that involve students in active, effortful work—practices including collaboration problem-solving . . . and community engagements" (AACU), but it also allows a prime environment to introduce skills needed for intercultural communication. College writing courses allow an excellent environment for practicing service learning assignments that introduce students to *collaboration* and *community engagement* within multicultural situations. Finally, this essay will discuss activities that encourage students to view arguments from their opposition's perspective to further promote skills needed for intercultural communication. These assignments can be incorporated separately or as a series in a composition classroom; it is my belief that if they are taught as a series, students who experience all these activities move from familiarity of others, to sympathy and social responsibility, and hopefully on towards full empathy for others.

When diversity is reflected upon in the composition classroom, the course dynamic tends to change a great deal. Students interact with one another more often; they tend to be mindful of peers' difficulties and often end up helping one another with course requirements. These multicultural opportunities give students vital intercultural skills that enable them to become more effective students in their various college disciplines, more desirable employees, and conscientious world citizens.

Learning *about* the *Other* through Interviewing

Composition courses are generally required for all college students; although this can serve as a challenge to instructors because of varying student ability and background in writing, composition courses present a unique opportunity. These courses most often assure a diverse student body; students usually differ in majors, but they also undoubtedly come from diverse cultures. Some students will come into composition courses speaking English as a second language, or as international students. This diversity, paired with the nature of writing courses, can create opportunities to explore, question, and research the impact of diversity and intercultural communication in an interdisciplinary context.

Gerald Graff in *Beyond the Culture Wars: How Teaching the Conflicts can Revitalize American Education* expresses the need for instructors to openly teach the conflicts that arise in contemporary society, but what is unique about Graff is that he promotes teaching conflicts that arise within the classroom. Open discussion of differences in the classroom is valued and needed for setting the foundational knowledge of intercultural communication. For instance, to ignore or continue on with the course without acknowledging the challenges some ESL students face in composition is a disservice to international students; likewise it is a disservice to American students to ignore that the course may at times be slowed down due to language issues. In this setting, it is helpful to openly discuss language and cultural differences that exist in the classroom; it is also valuable to include assignments that allow students to learn from each other about their differences, so that acceptance and understanding of diversity will become part of the classroom.

Effective interview skills are an important part of the research process and encourage students to write about topics that are unrelated to themselves. An activity that can be used in composition courses to help break perceived barriers is to assign students a paper where they interview an international student in their class or on campus about his or her background, so that the process of interviewing this student about his or her culture becomes an opportunity to be introduced to diversity and multiculturalism. Students should be paired with an international student they do not yet know; they should then conduct a brief interview asking general questions about their interviewee, including questions related to his or her cultural background. This first interview mainly serves as an opportunity for students to get to know each other. Students are usually a bit reticent to conduct these interviews, mainly because of a fear of language barriers. In my class, we spend time discussing techniques to prepare for conducting an interview with someone who may speak English as a second language; we discuss the importance of active listening and putting the interviewee at ease through receptive nonverbal language cues. Every time I teach this assignment, it is surprising how fast students become comfortable speaking with one another. Students consistently state that their fears of an inability to communicate immediately dissipated because they were prepared to overcome small language misunderstandings and entered the process with a willingness to engage in a dialogue.

After the first interview, students should then have time to research their interviewee's background, so that a second interview will be more comprehensive. Students can ask more pointed questions directed towards their paper topic, such as implicit and explicit cultural traditions, rules, and beliefs. Students can also use this opportunity to ask issues relating to cultural ethics and morality, and how the interviewee feels he or she fits his or her culture's principles. Usually when I teach this assignment, I ask students to ask their interviewee to answer questions first in their native language, and then state their response again in English. I also suggest that the last ten minutes of the interview be comprised of the interviewee teaching the interviewer some words in his or her language; I stress that the student should repeatedly attempt to say each word until the interviewee feels it is correct. I feel it is important for students to hear another language that they may be unfamiliar with in a dialogue setting and have the experience of trying to speak a few words of the language to a native speaker of the language, so that students understand a small portion of the interview subject's international student experience.

Finally, the students should be expected to construct an informational paper about the interview subject and his or her culture. Students should also incorporate a persuasive purpose of the importance of diversity within their greater college community by including not only a summary about what they have learned from their interviewee but also a discussion of what they specifically learned from participating in this project, including the effectiveness of their initial plan to communicate in an intercultural experience, and whether they had to adapt any of their communication techniques to promote a more successful interview. Students should also discuss their overall experience listening to their interviewee's native language, and also their attempt to speak the language, as they ponder the experience of studying as an international student. They should also include a moment of introspection about what they learned about their interviewee's values and culture that they did not previously know, and a discussion of any of their own personal beliefs or preconceptions that changed because of their experience with their interview subject. Finally, they should conclude with how this experience they had provides evidence that others should pursue intercultural experiences across college disciplines through extending a hand in friendship, studying abroad, traveling, research, etc.

Class discussion about learning outcomes is essential to the success of this project. Also, a general discussion about the importance of multiculturalism and diversity in all college disciplines is needed throughout the project, so that students may carry their discoveries to their various disciplines. Initially discussion of differences in the classroom and the challenges students face because of their differences can be difficult, but once the project comes to an end, the classroom dynamic changes a great deal. After the project, I consistently find that students are often more willing to discuss issues relating to diversity and are also seemingly more compassionate and understanding toward one another. In addition, they tend to work more readily with each other to understand assignments and course expectations. Again, this assignment provides a platform for students to obtain a meaningful experience of being introduced to another of diverse background.

Experience *with* the *Other* in Service Learning

Again, service learning opportunities within composition classrooms enable students to gain intercultural communication skills that are highly desirable by many employers, as real-world applications of communication across multicultural boundaries is an applied skill that many college students have not sufficiently met upon graduation (AACU). Service learning opportunities in the composition classroom takes the introduction to diversity to another level by increasing a student's sense of sympathy for others and social responsibility, bridging the use of applied intercultural skills towards an examination of the noted AACU's employer value of "ethical judgment and integrity."

Much research indicates that student acceptance and understanding of diversity is a benefit of service learning: "Service-learning produces a number of positive effects on college students . . . includ[ing] a . . . reduction of stereotypes and better cultural understanding; and development of interpersonal skills, citizenship, social responsibility, critical thinking, and connectedness to college and career" (Worrell-Carlisle 198). Through service learning projects, young writers achieve some of the highest goals college instructors want their students to obtain; they interact with diverse groups of people and often create a project that is centered on a subject matter that was initially unfamiliar to them. They learn skills to cope in a real-world setting, as well as see the advantage of creating an assignment that has a concrete benefit for others. Through service learning activities writers also enact with others of diverse cultures and will enter into experiences that allow them to begin to commiserate with people different than themselves:

> Because service encourages students to see themselves as intimately connected to the other, a learning context is created in

which the caring self is more likely to emerge. Fostering a sense
of self grounded in an ethic of care is one of the central challenges of education and becomes increasingly important as our
society grows more diverse. By fostering an ethic of care, higher
education encourages the sense of otherness needed for democracy to service and, indeed, thrive in a complex and fragmented
social world. (Rhoads 294)

Composition students can take part in myriad types of service learning projects, I especially feel it is useful to create projects that incorporate interview skills
within community service. For example, students can generate local history
through interviews of different residents of their community and later publish
these papers ("101 Ideas" 5). This service of writing and dissemination of their
material benefits students through the interaction they receive with other community members, teaching them a great deal about the different cultural elements
within their own community, but it also becomes a service to the larger community because the published papers continue to educate myriad members of the
community on a topic that may have gone unnoticed. In addition, community
service projects helps students understand the many types of diversity that exist
within and sustain a community. Projects should be created to immerse the student in a largely unknown cultural environment than that of his or her previous
experience; this can be actualized through introducing students to local groups
with a clear cultural focus, such as a local American Indian community. Also,
the definition of diversity should be considered through such projects as well, as
service learning projects that examine age, gender, sexuality, etc. in the context
of diversity can also be beneficial, as many employers again value applied skills
that enable employees to effectively and ethically communicate in various diverse
situations. For example, a service learning project that focuses on age as a form
of diversity and introduces students to a generation different from their own will
provide students with applied, cross-generational, communication skills that will
meet the needs of many career settings.

In my composition courses, I have students interview residents of a local
nursing home about their childhoods and record the stories for preservation
efforts of the community. My students write children's books from the childhood
stories provided by the elderly residents, and then they visit an elementary school
class where an elementary student illustrates the book. At the end of the project
all involved participants meet to read the book and celebrate this accomplishment. This project has proved effective because students learn the importance of
capturing stories from an older generation and imparting them to a younger generation. This project is also beneficial because it naturally addresses issues related
to diversity; students are given the opportunity to listen to and interact with those
of various ages, social class, race, cultural background, etc. Students involved in
this project also can grasp the importance of history. This service learning project

allows student to capture the local historical stories within their current community from the older residents of the nursing home and pass them on to a younger generation, so that these stories do not become forgotten. Finally, students can be challenged to connect the messages or morals of their children's books towards themes of embracing diversity, preserving history, and learning about others; therefore, this project, if the assignments in this paper are taught together as a series, expands upon the skills students obtained in their interviews with international students to more defined experiences of interacting with others for a clear purpose of preserving local history, thus the student, through this project begins to understand the importance of personal responsibility. In addition, I ask students upon completion of this project to write another persuasive paper, with the purpose now of arguing for the value of diversity awareness in the greater community and workforce. Much like their interview paper that examined the process they underwent to interact with an international, this paper largely should focus on the student's reflection of the process, but should finally achieve an argument for carrying the lessons of this project to their future careers.

Elaine Norris in "Age Matters in a Feminist Classroom" discusses a writing project where her class also interviewed elderly residents of a nursing home about issues relating to feminism. The class read many essays that dealt with feminist issues, but it was the actual experience of interviewing these residents about first hand stories of what it was like to live in previous eras that provided an invaluable element. Students also gained perspective on the residents' views of feminism today. In addition, ageism naturally became an issue of discussion and reflection. Norris states that this experience:

> transformed our relationships with people. . . . We engaged in learning with our senior partners as interwoven subjects of knowledge. . . . Taking on perspectives of age and of each senior partner specifically prevented us from turning our . . . learning into a self-serving patronizing experience that is ageist and inconsistent with feminist principles. (79)

There are many other service learning projects that can further offer students experiences with the importance of personal responsibility towards others. Service learning can also allow faces and names to be connected to real human rights issues: "immersing themselves in a real world environment helps [students] to see the complexity of situations faced by the people with whom they interact" (Krain & Nurse 193). Robert A. Rhoads in his "In the Service of Citizenship" discusses how the service learning project he conducted in his classroom "forced [his] students to confront generalizations they had of the other. For example, students talked about various stereotypes they held about poor people and how such stereotypes were erased as a result of their service work" (288). Michael D. Mcnally in "Indigenous Pedagogy in the Classroom" suggests an interview project that involves reading historical pieces that portray the American Indian in racist terms and then visiting with members of a local American Indian tribe to hear a modernized perspective: "Unlearning racism can seldom if ever happen through book learning and essay writing alone" (606). Mcnally states that these types of firsthand service learning encounters with the *other* tend to "engineer jarring experiences that stir up the tidiness of categories carried deep within students' minds" (606). It is precisely the process of having students encounter the *other* on a personal level that serves as a transformative experience for them.

Again, after students partake in the initial interaction with their service learning partners, they should carry these various projects further by writing a persuasive piece that carries the specific project goals to a broader discussion of the importance of diversity within their community, workplace, and the world at large. These papers could be designed to ask readers to reevaluate such issues as feminism, ageism, and racism, and advocate an action step to their readers; for instance, students could visit a local homeless shelter, interview and observe some residents, and then write a persuasive paper advocating others to donate or assist at a local homeless shelter within their own community.

Rhoads contends that "A significant learning experience associated with community service was the opportunity to better understand the lives students worked to serve. Students were able to put faces and names with the alarming statistics and endless policy debates about homelessness as well as rural and urban poverty" (287). When students join in the work of a nonprofit, for example, and write about it as an insider, they create a sense of shared mission that gets them past the *us v. them* mentality that tends to limit our interactions with groups of which we don't feel ourselves a part. Listening carefully to these stories of others can not only create an acceptance of the *other*, but it may also lead the student to change his or her own previous views. Once again, the class discussion and written assignments that follows these projects is as essential as the project itself. Open dialogue and then written reflection of both the process of interviewing and the feelings and preconceived notions they may have had before beginning the project helps students better grasp the benefit and necessity of personal responsibility to not only learn about those who may be different from oneself but also to feel an obligation of personal responsibility towards issues relating to diversity within their various college disciplines, workplaces, and personal lives.

Experience *as* the *Other* through Oppositional Exercises

The first two assignments presented in this chapter discussed their goals of providing students the means to learn about those of other cultures and belief systems through interviews, as well as moving on to encourage feelings of sympathy and responsibility towards others through service learning. These goals are important for students to gain an understanding and commiseration of others, but this final activity asks students to further incorporate these intercultural skills by attempting to briefly become their perceived *other*.

The inclusion of the opposition's arguments is always important to any persuasive paper in composition. Ideally, students should incorporate a fair and accurate assessment of the opposition's arguments into papers, but realistically, the logical soundness, accuracy, and fairness of these arguments are often inadequate. Students frequently find it difficult to include detailed oppositional arguments in their papers because they often have a hard time grasping the viewpoint of the *other*. When composition students learn the art of persuasive writing, they learn to become familiar with their opposition's arguments, so they can present and then refute their opposition and then continue on to persuade their audience of their thesis. Arguably, seeking an understanding of their opposition only in order to defeat their points may not be enough to gain an adequate knowledge of the viewpoints of those who disagree with them. Therefore, this assignment encourages students to become, in a sense, their own opposition. This project asks students to take on the viewpoints of their opposition in an in-class debate.

Students first research their opposition's three major arguments against the point of view in their own thesis. To start the students of the class should represent their persuasive thesis to the class. Then the student, now in the role of their own opposition, should present these three oppositional arguments to the class. The rest of the class is then asked to enter into a debate as proponents of the student's original persuasive viewpoint, so the only member representing the opposition will be the student presenter. The student needs to defend his or her opposition's viewpoints to a class of dissenters as if the arguments were his or her own personal viewpoints.

Students initially find this activity difficult, as defending a contrary view to your original beliefs to a whole class of dissenters in not an easy task; it is hard for students to argue from the perspective of their own opposition in the extensive way this activity requires. Many students state their three oppositional arguments very briefly, and when presented with a class of dissenters who are expressing the student's original stance in order to invalidate these oppositional points, the student presenters tend to repeatedly state that they do not agree with these points, so they can't defend them. I like to use this opportunity, which almost always arises in the first few students who present, to express my understanding that it is a difficult assignment. I then tell students that we do this exercise exactly because students find it very hard to accurately and clearly state a belief system that differs from their own, but I restate that academic persuasive papers need to have a strong oppositional component, so that the refutation of these tenets will make the paper even stronger. Moreover, when I teach this assignment, I try to make it a light atmosphere; I laugh a lot and help the students when they stumble in trying to defend their new position as their own opposition. The class, as dissenters, and each as presenters in waiting, picks up on the light and helpful atmosphere and tends to help each other as well. If student presenters are struggling to back up arguments, I often ask the class and the student to switch roles for a moment; the class then becomes a large group of the student's opposition, and the student gets to defend his or her original position, while taking notes of the points the classmates come up with. This switching of roles also helps students to understand that positions vary among individuals; any argument will always have opponents, and one must be mindful of a diverse audience that represents a wide array of views.

Again, as with all of the assignments discussed in this chapter, classroom dialog should explore the importance of understanding, accepting, and possibly even being changed by the *other*. The struggle that these students go through with this activity provides a great opportunity to discuss the importance of knowing and learning about one's opposition in a thorough way. Only writing briefly about one's opposition does not often allow students to have to apply their opposition's position. Oftentimes, at the close of this oppositional assignment, students end up changing their initial persuasive stance and adopting the arguments of their opposition; this opportunity for change is highly beneficial to the student, and it is one that can serve as a life lesson.

I once had a student who stated that he came from a household where gay marriage, the subject of his persuasive paper, was intolerable; he easily wrote the first draft of his paper defending his thesis against gay marriage. He struggled a great deal with the opposition assignment; he had brief oppositional points, but could not defend the arguments to the class as his own opposition. He stated that he couldn't do the assignment because he did not agree with these views. I stated that agreeing with the views was not the point of the assignment; the purpose was to accurately reflect the views, so that he could refute a clear and accurate opposition. When he still struggled, I asked the class to switch roles and became the opposition of his paper. He furiously began taking notes of the classes arguments they presented to him for gay marriage. Interestingly, I found that this student now struggled to defend his original position to the class. He came up to me the next class period and asked if it would be a problem for him to switch sides in his paper. He said that he was not convinced that his own views on gay marriage had changed, but that the opposition assignment got him thinking about the beliefs of other people. He stated that he thought it would be good for him to try to write the whole paper from the perspective of someone in support of gay marriage. And at the end of the term, his paper indeed was written from this changed perspective. I believe that the paper was quite strong because both his side, in support of gay marriage, and now his opposition's side, against gay marriage, provided clear, accurate representations of this topic, and more so, I felt this change in, at the very least, his willingness to try to explore the views of people opposed to his own beliefs, provided him an invaluable lesson in diversity.

Composition courses allow excellent opportunities for students to learn about and interact with a broad range of diverse people, whether it is with other classmates or members of their community, in order to obtain applied intercultural skills valued by employers. The introduction of these assignments promotes an ideal first step towards understanding diversity. Again, these assignments can be taught separately, but when taught as a series, they allow students the experience of carrying this first introduction of diversity to the next level of ethical awareness by contemplating, discussing, and producing material that enables students to move towards elements of empathy and social responsibility, and on towards a willingness to be changed by the *other*, so they come to welcome diverse viewpoints in their myriad college disciplines, careers, and personal lives.

Works Cited

Association of American Colleges and Universities. *It Takes More Than a Major: Employer Priorities for College Learning and Student Success.* Washington, DC, Wednesday 22 November 2014.

Florida International University Library. "101 Ideas for Combining Service and Learning." *Florida International University Library,* 2006, www.fiu.edu/~time4chg /Library/ideas.html.

Krain, Matthew, and Anne M. Nurse. "Teaching Human Rights through Service Learning." *Human Rights Quarterly,* vol. 26, no. 1, 2004, pp. 189–207.

Mcnally, Michael D. "Indigenous Pedagogy in the Classroom: A Service Learning Model for Discussion." *The American Indian Quarterly,* vol. 28, no. 3, 2004, pp. 604–617.

Norris, Elaine. "Age Matters in a Feminist Classroom." *NWSA Journal,* vol. 18, no. 1, 2006, pp. 61–84.

Rhoads, Robert A. "In the Service of Citizenship: A Study of Student Involvement in Community Service." *The Journal of Higher Education,* vol. 69, no. 3, May–June 1998, pp. 277–297.

Worrell-Carlisle, Pamela J. "Service-Learning: A Tool for Developing Cultural Awareness." *Nurse Educator,* vol. 30, no. 5, 2005, pp. 197–202.

Chapter 6. Influence of the College Composition Classroom on Students' Values and Beliefs

Ruth A. Goldfine and Deborah Mixson-Brookshire
KENNESAW STATE UNIVERSITY

When composing essays for their college composition class, students often reveal their values and beliefs, particularly when they must take—and defend—a position in persuasive essays. The ability of students to not only state their position on an issue but also to clearly articulate—and defend—the rationale for that position is part of their ethical development that occurs during the college years as they become autonomous adults. Moreover, possessing a clarity of perspective, a rationale for that perspective, and the capability to articulate both can greatly contribute to students' success both in college and in their professional lives.

While many first-year students in a composition class may find it easy to state their position on issues, they often struggle to provide the rationale for those positions. That is, while they know *what* they believe, they don't seem certain of *why* they believe it.

On what, then, do they base their beliefs? While it may seem logical to assume that students, particularly traditional-age first-year college students, have simply adopted the values and beliefs of their parents, a review of the literature revealed little research to support or disprove this assumption.

What the research did reveal was that, even when challenged to examine and support their values and beliefs, students who have an established position on an issue are not likely to critique their position or consider alternatives (Perkins 568). However, a single experience with one student in a first-year composition classroom that contradicted this expectation led us to conduct a pilot study to examine the genesis of students' values and beliefs, and to assess the influence of the college composition class on those values and beliefs.

Several years ago, PJ (a pseudonym), a traditional-age student in my college composition class, chose the controversy over the Georgia state flag as the topic of his persuasive essay. At that time, a public debate over the existing "stars and bars" design was quite prominent, pitting those who advocated changing the flag's design based on the argument that the "stars and bars" was representative of 1950s-era discrimination (Dembner F11; Rankin C8; Schmukler 34) against those who viewed the flag as a distinctive symbol of their Southern heritage and, therefore, opposed any change to it.

PJ fell into the latter group and planned to write a persuasive essay arguing in favor of maintaining the flag's existing design. When he submitted his final paper at the end of the semester, the essay offered a thorough and detailed argument in favor of *changing* the design of the Georgia state flag—a position completely opposite of that he had defended in class discussions at the start of the semester. He later explained that the findings of his research had led him to question his beliefs and the evidence had persuaded him to reconsider his position.

That PJ learned much about his topic through the research he conducted was not surprising. Numerous researchers have found that writing can influence learning, noting that "writing is a powerful means of learning" (Gere 2) and "a unique way of knowing and . . . reaching understanding" (Fulwiler x). What *was* surprising was the dramatic change in PJ's position on the issue of the Georgia state flag in just a few short months. PJ clearly defies Perkins' finding that students are not likely to critique the positions they hold, and, in fact, PJ's shift in perspective may represent the type of personal growth that writing and the composition classroom *could*—and maybe should—foster.

That such a profound shift in belief is possible through the writing process has been promoted and supported by numerous researchers. For example, Toby Fulwiler argues that we "write to ourselves as well as talk with others to objectify our perceptions of reality . . . to order and represent our own understanding. In this sense, language . . . becomes a tool for discovering, for shaping meaning" (Fulwiler x). Similarly, Syrene Forsman contends that writing instructors can make a conscious choice to facilitate students' ability to think rather than "sentencing [them] to thoughtless mechanical operations" and believes that students who are "encouraged to try a variety of thought processes in classes . . . [can] develop considerable mental power" (162). But perhaps it is Barbara Walvoord who gives voice to the most elevated expectations of writing, choosing to view writing skills as a "climbing rope whereby students can hoist themselves to the next level of intellectual maturity" (5)—an intellectual maturity demonstrated by PJ when he altered his belief based on the evidence he found. He could now articulate the *why* behind his belief.

The profound shift in perspective that PJ underwent after extensive research suggests he experienced in-depth learning and demonstrates that he was able to synthesize information into an informed position on the issue. However, this shift also calls into question the genesis of PJ's original position. That is, since the available evidence led him to support changing the design of the Georgia state flag, it seems likely that his original position opposing the change was not based on available evidence but rather shaped by other influences.

To better understand the influences that may shape the beliefs and values of PJ and other college composition students, we conducted a pilot study of 11 traditional-age first-year students enrolled in a second-semester Honors English composition course at a large public university. In this course, students spent the semester focused on academic research and argumentation in the production of documented persuasive essays.

As part of the study, we administered surveys (at the start and end of the semester) that asked students to rank a list of values, to state their position on the issues they had ranked, and to indicate who or what had influenced their values and beliefs. Additionally, we conducted one-on-one discussions with students throughout the semester, invited them to participate in an end-of-the-semester interview (offered as either a face-to-face option or an email interview), and conducted an analysis of students' papers as they progressed from their initial drafts to the final versions of those essays.

Several limitations affected the outcome of this study. The greatest of these limitations was the small number of participants. Since the participants were part of an Honors section of English composition, the class size was intentionally limited to 15 students. Of these, three were ineligible to participate in the study because they were under the age of 18. Furthermore, only 11 of the 12 eligible students chose to complete the survey at the start of the semester, and of those 11, only two attempted the end-of-the-semester survey but neither completed it in its entirety. Finally, although several students indicated a willingness to participate in end-of-semester interviews, only one ultimately participated. Thus, while we were able to identify the values of students at the start of the semester, there was insufficient data from the end-of-semester surveys to allow us to conclusively determine if any shift in students' values occurred during the course of the semester.

A second limitation was that participants ranked only those values listed on the research instrument and did not add any additional values, even though they were invited to do so. Consequently, the results represent only the ranking of those values presented by the researchers although additional values of importance to the participants may exist.

Finally, since the students were fairly homogenous academically (all were Honors students), roughly the same age (18–19), and mostly female (9 of the 11), our findings should not be seen as representative of all college composition students but rather suggest avenues for future research.

In the surveys, students were asked to rank eight values from most to least important. Those values were religion/spirituality, health, financial stability, security, knowledge, family, sense of belonging, and friends. The three values that were rated most important by a majority of students were, in order from most to least important, (1) family, (2) religion/spirituality, and (3) sense of belonging. The least important values were (6) knowledge, (7) health, and (8) friends. Figure 6.1 indicates the percentage of students that ranked each of the eight values as most important or least important to them. For example, the table shows that nearly 90% of the students surveyed ranked *family* as one of their most important values, while 50% of the respondents claimed that *friends* ranked as one of their least important values.

Students were also asked to indicate which of 19 current issues were of greatest concern to them personally; as a neutral response, students could indicate that they had insufficient knowledge to understand an issue. Open-ended questions invited students to share their views and/or positions on these issues. Figure 6.2 provides a complete listing of the issues that were presented to students and shows the percentage of student respondents who *strongly agree/agree* or *disagree/ strongly disagree* that the issue cited is of concern to them.

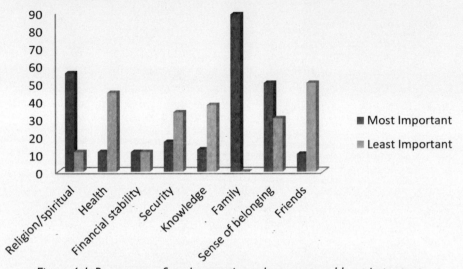

Figure 6.1. Percentage of students rating values most and least important

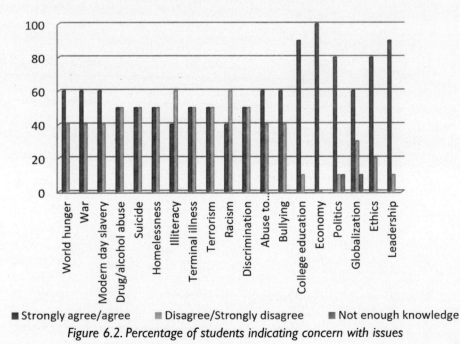

Figure 6.2. Percentage of students indicating concern with issues

The issue of greatest concern to participants in this study was the economy, with a full 100% of the students *strongly agreeing/agreeing* that this was an issue of concern to them, and nearly 90% *strongly agreeing/agreeing* that both a college education and leadership was important to them. For the majority of the remaining issues, 50%-60% of participants *strongly agreed/agreed* that these issues were of concern. Two notable exceptions were illiteracy and racism; for both of these, only 40% of participants *strongly agreed/agreed* that these issues were of concern.

The open-ended questions asking students for their opinion/position on each issue resulted in a wide range of responses. For three of the 19 issues—illiteracy, terminal illness, and politics—participants provided no comments or positions. The remaining 16 issues received from one to five comments each, several of which stated participants' positions/views on the issues, such as:

- War is inevitable, so we must be ready to fight. (War)
- I don't think that drugs such as marijuana should be legalized. (Drug/Alcohol Abuse)
- There should be a cap to the unemployment checks. (Homelessness)
- Everyone is entitled to a college education. (College Education)

Other comments were simply observations or judgments rather than actual views/positions on an issue:

- People starve everyday while we eat ten Big Macs per day. (World Hunger)
- I work with an organization that strives to help people with suicidal tendencies. (Suicide)
- Colorblind for the win! (Racism)
- Boo Mike Vick. (Abuse to Humans/Animals)
- I am currently in college. (College Education)

In response to the open-ended question regarding the factors or individuals that influenced the development of their views and positions on the various issues, students most often cited parents and teachers as having the greatest impact.

Only one student participated in the end-of-semester email interview that asked open-ended questions designed to gauge whether the participants' values remained consistent throughout the semester and to identify those factors that shaped their values and positions on the various issues. The interviewee indicated that her values remained consistent throughout the semester but that, through her composition class, she came to understand "the importance of basing arguments in current, scientific data, as well as how media can skew certain issues and greatly sway public opinion." Regarding those influences that shaped her views, the respondent wrote:

> I have been profoundly influenced by the authority figures in
> my life. It is their wisdom and life experiences that have shaped
> the paradigm that I have. My parents, pastors, and certain key

teachers have helped me develop a worldview that causes me to have many similar opinions on issues such as economic structures, religious choice, and political orientation. I am not ashamed to say that I would probably follow very closely with their beliefs and opinions if they were presented to me.

This participant further indicated that:

it is important to have a founded worldview from which you draw positions on current issues. If your opinions flow from a tested, challenged, yet stronger worldview, they will have continuity and you will be able to defend the positions you take. Without a stance on issues that face society, it is impossible to call for change. At times, though, you must be able to yield to authorities who you trust have more informed opinions and reference them when you realize that you simply do not have the knowledge to substantiate your own opinion on issues.

An analysis of the participants' writing and the one-on-one discussions conducted with students revealed that a majority of participants maintained the same position on the issue they were researching from the first draft through the final version. The two exceptions were CH and HS. CH was interested in piracy on the Internet, particularly free music downloads (of which she was in favor). Her first draft was a strictly informative essay in which she explored the evolution of the music industry and current music downloading practices. As she struggled to develop a thesis and identify claims for her persuasive essay, CH had great difficulty defining piracy and even greater difficulty developing claims and locating documented evidence in support of free music downloads. Consequently, CH changed her thesis when, based on her research, she concluded that the Internet was of greater benefit to small bands trying to gain a following than it was to larger, well-established bands. Therefore, her final persuasive paper argued in favor of free music downloading as a means for small bands to gain wider visibility and increase their fan base.

HS had a similar experience in drafting his essay. Much like CH, he had identified a topic (AIDS/HIV) and wrote a first draft that was informative and exploratory. However, the topic proved too broad, and he decided to narrow his focus to a particular aspect of AIDS/HIV. In the second draft of his paper, HS refined his essay to include a clearly stated thesis: "Today's laws regarding HIV/AIDS need to be reevaluated. Some are outdated, some need to be altered, and still others need to be created." One of the laws HS identified as being in need of change prohibited homosexual males from donating blood. In his paper, HS argued that advanced testing methods for screening blood make this law obsolete and unnecessary, stating, "The blood is screened using very accurate tests, reducing the risk of tainted blood to virtually zero." While he makes a valid point, this is the extent of the evidence he offered in support of changing the law regarding homosexual blood donors. However, in the conclusion of his essay, he wrote: "Archaic laws, such as being unable to donate blood, greatly diminish the blood supply and discriminate against certain groups." That this statement does not appear until the final paragraph of his paper suggests that he may have drawn this conclusion as a result of the writing process itself by reflecting on the sources he had gathered and synthesizing that material into a coherent position on the issue.

The remaining study participants developed thesis statements in their original drafts that articulated their position on an issue, and they maintained that position throughout the semester. While these students easily stated their positions based on the knowledge they already possessed, they had difficulty identifying claims and locating evidence to support those positions. For example, in the first draft of her essay, BK began with the thesis, "Nurses need to work shorter shifts to protect themselves and their patients and coworkers." While she was firm in her conviction, BK's limited knowledge on the subject led her to speculate on possible claims to support her thesis. When her attempts to find evidence in support of her speculative claims proved difficult, she was forced to rethink her thesis.

While our intent was to compare students' rankings of their values at the start of the semester with those at the end of the semester, the poor rate of return on the post-test surveys did not allow for any meaningful comparative analysis. However, the data we were able to collect offered some valuable insight.

Given the age of the participants, their ranking of values was unremarkable (for example, all participants ranked *family* as most important), with the possible exception of *friends*, which was ranked least important of all the values listed. This seems to contradict the importance they place on *sense of belonging*, which ranked third, although one might conclude that their *sense of belonging* is derived through family (the highest ranked value) rather than friends. Alternatively, they may have viewed *friends* as being encompassed by *sense of belonging* and did not regard *friends* as a wholly separate value. Given that *friends* ranked so low among the participants, and that this was unexpected given the age of the respondents, this finding may not be indicative of the values of most first-year college students. Further study is warranted before any definitive conclusions can be drawn.

In addition to ranking their values, students were asked to indicate which current issues, from a list of 19, were of concern to them. Eight of the issues were not of concern to 50% of the respondents; these were *drug/alcohol abuse, suicide, homelessness, illiteracy, terminal illness, terrorism, racism,* and *discrimination.* This is not surprising given that, based on the demographic of the participants, it is likely that none of these issues affected them directly. Conversely, *economy, college education,* and *leadership* were rated as issues of concern by 100%, 90%, and 90% of the study participants, respectively. However, the comments they provided suggest a superficial understanding of these issues that belies their purported level of concern. Only one respondent provided a comment on *economy,* and this was a statement of fact rather than an actual position: "It is hard to find work." Regarding *college education*, two of the three responses provided could be loosely defined as positions on the issue: "Everyone is entitled to a college education" and "It's important." The other response was simply a statement of fact: "I am currently in college." Finally, regarding *leadership*, only one respondent provided a position on the issue: "Our country needs better leaders and role models."

Finally, though a majority of students (60%) indicated that *racism, globalization,* and *world hunger* were of concern to them, the comments they provided when asked to state their position on the issues raise some doubts regarding the depth and seriousness of their concern—as well as the extent of their knowledge about these issues. For example, student responses included such statements as, "There isn't racism anymore. We have a black president," as well as "Why are people in India taking American jobs?" and "People starve everyday while we eat ten Big Macs per day."

Our research indicates that first-year composition students have a clear sense of their values and often have positions on many of today's issues but generally lack the knowledge and life experience to articulate the reasons for the beliefs they hold. Additionally, what knowledge they do possess regarding the issues may be rudimentary or superficial, limiting their ability to develop their opinions wholly separate from those held by the authority figures in their lives. Consequently, it would seem that either their beliefs and opinions may be poorly formed because of a simplistic understanding of an issue or they have merely adopted the opinions and views of influential adults in their lives, such as parents or teachers. Finally, the evolution of thought apparent in the drafts of their papers suggests that the research and reflection necessary when writing an essay for a college composition class can lead to the acquisition of new knowledge, a questioning of values/beliefs, and the development of a student's own voice.

Since teachers were cited among those authority figures whose opinions influenced students' values and beliefs, it is possible that what takes place in the composition classroom could potentially impact the values of students, particularly since writing can be viewed as "a value-forming activity, a means of finding our voice as well as making our voice heard . . . [and] this value-forming activity is perhaps the most personally and socially significant role writing plays in our education" (Fulwiler x). Therefore, instructors should be intentional in the manner in which they guide students through the writing process in order to provide opportunities for students to form their values and find their voices.

For example, composition instructors can identify and introduce for class discussion controversial issues of interest to students. Such discussions can reveal a tremendous diversity of thought and attitudes regarding current events or hotly debated topics. Consequently, in order to ensure such discussions remain civil and productive, instructors must demand that students respect one another's viewpoints and comport themselves appropriately. Instructors should also take care to remain neutral on these issues so that students are free to form their own conclusions without being influenced by the instructors' personal views.

Additionally, students should be required to research the issues thoroughly, locating and considering supporting evidence—from valid, reputable sources—for both sides of an issue, thereby offering students the opportunity to synthesize the evidence and develop their own perspective on the topic. Requiring students to write multiple drafts of an essay that incorporates this evidence will demand that they repeatedly reconsider the issue (and evidence) and may lead to the levels of understanding and intellectual maturity of which Fulwiler and Walvoord spoke.

Finally, composition students might be challenged to write a persuasive essay in support of a position that is directly opposite of the one they actually hold. In challenging them to make an argument in support of a belief they oppose, instructors can help students take a fresh look at the available evidence, evaluate the overwhelming amount of information made available through technological advances, and perhaps gain an understanding of the rationale of "the other side."

Most first-year students come to college fresh from high school with clear values and beliefs. However, while these students may know *what* they believe, they are often unable to articulate *why*. While it may not be common for first-year composition students to experience a dramatic shift in opinion during the course of one semester in the composition classroom, the fact that it occurred in the instance of PJ demonstrates the profound impact a first-year composition course can have. Through the process of researching and writing in their college composition courses, some students may finally be able to articulate *why* they believe as they do, while others may for the first time adopt a position on an issue as an entity wholly separate from their parents, making their initial forays into the adult world and forging their identities as individuals.

If composition instructors choose to embrace the notion that the goal of college is to "encourage each student to develop the capacity to judge wisely in matters of life and conduct ... [and] set [students] free in a world of ideas and provide a climate in which ethical and moral choices can be thoughtfully examined, and convictions formed" (Halloran 61), and if they seek the means to promote such development, the composition classroom has the potential to promote personal growth, to provide students the opportunity to find their own voices, and to facilitate intellectual maturity.

Works Cited

Dembner, Alice. "Georgia Flag Sparks Protest." *Boston Globe*, 20 July 1996, p. F11.

Forsman, Syrene. "Writing to Learn Means Learning to Think." *Roots in the Sawdust: Writing to Learn Across the Disciplines*, edited by Anne Ruggles Gere. National Council of Teachers of English, 1985, pp. 162–174.

Fulwiler, Toby. Introduction. *Language Connections: Writing and Reading Across the Curriculum*, edited by Toby Fulwiler and Art Young. National Council of Teachers of English, 1982.

Gere, Anne Ruggles. Introduction. *Roots in the Sawdust: Writing to Learn Across the Disciplines*, edited by Anne Ruggles Gere. National Council of Teachers of English, 1985, pp. 1–8.

Halloran, S. Michael. "Aristotle's Concept of Ethos, or if not His Somebody Else's." *Rhetoric Review,* vol. 1, no. 1, 1982, pp. 58–63.

Perkins, D. N. "Postprimary Education has Little Impact on Informal Reasoning." *Journal of Educational Psychology*, vol. 77, no. 5, 1985, pp. 562–571.

Rankin, Bill. "Judge Rejects Suit Against State Flag." *The Atlanta Journal-Constitution,* 4 Jan. 1996, p. C8.

Schmukler, Evelina. "Georgia Flag Protested." *New York Times,* 20 July 1996, p. 34.

Walvoord, Barbara E. *Helping Students Write Well: A Guide for Teachers in All Disciplines,* 2nd ed. The Modern Language Association of America, 1986.

Section 2: How We Write

Chapter 7. Introduction

Renée Love
LANDER UNIVERSITY

Writing processes are as unique and varied as we are as writers. I have been practicing as a writing teacher for over 23 years, (and as a writer longer), but every
semester I learn more about how we write and how to teach others to write, and
so I revise my *lines* so that in the next class, I can better motivate the *whole writer*
and perhaps the writing *dance* might be more soulful. We likely all have favorite
best practices in writing instruction, but the next time you are planning a writing
course or revising an assignment, I hope you will also consider some of the interdisciplinary approaches shared in this chapter. The writing process, the space for
learning, and the students we teach, defy easy categorizations that suggest "one
type fits all," a lesson my students taught me many semesters ago.

I was teaching at a large agriculture and engineering school, an environment with few liberal arts majors, and it seemed more likely that I would win the
Powerball jackpot than encounter an English major in any of my classes. I was
deep into grading a batch of essays about stereotypes. Many of the papers seemed
reminiscent of the movie *The Breakfast Club*—in the sense that students were
asked to reflect on the misconceptions of stereotypes. Some students approached
the assignment by examining and then deconstructing labels that had been
applied to them over the years, labels that reduced a person to a single word
like "jock," "nerd," "prep," "geek," and so on. I remember reading a paper that
sounded something like this: "There are many types of stereos: Sony, Yamaha,
Bose." I initially despaired, thinking *How could this student get the assignment so
wrong?* Thankfully, I continued reading and discovered that the young writer had
developed an insightful metaphor about stereos and some of the associations that
we have with various brands of electronics, and then he went on to apply those
concepts to human beings and how we may construct identities based on the
exterior, shallow experiences rather than on true understanding. The essay was
the best one in the class, and the student must have been like the one described in
Mina Shaughnessy's essay, "Diving In," when she quotes Leo Strauss. Shaughnessy
writes that we should "Always assume that there is one silent student in your class
who is by far superior to you in head and in heart" (98–99). I have met this student many times, in many different classrooms over the years, someone who, as
Shaughnessy puts it, is far superior in head and heart than I am.

I will never forget that paper or that student. I think he was an engineering
major, too. In reflecting on how we write, I am reading the "Stereotype" essay as
a metaphor about the uniqueness and wonder of our students, as well as the processes related to writing instruction. For veteran writing teachers, we may some-

times have knee-jerk reactions about how we *should* teach writing, thinking that one approach *fits most*, just as I did when I almost dismissed my student's "stereo" paper, thinking it was completely off base. But there are many "right" methods for writing instruction, many *writing pathways* that create opportunities for student success. How we teach writing is a question that spans across majors and touches many disciplines; we must adapt our approaches to meet these diverse contexts and purposes, as well as the diverse needs of our student populations. In this section, writers share several pedagogical methods for teaching writing, suggesting how we can enrich students' learning experiences by using a holistic, affective pedagogy in writing classes; how writing instruction methods might borrow from other disciplines, including theatre and dance; and even how team teaching and mentoring strategies can benefit not only our students but new teachers.

The chapter begins with Rachel Anya Dearie Fomalhaut's discussion of affective pedagogies, entitled "Holistic Learning for Real-Life Writers: A Call for Affective Pedagogy in First-Year Composition." Fomaalhaut's "propose[s] that we, as teachers, more intentionally engage the affective spheres of our classrooms, whether traditional brick-and-mortar or online." By affective, Fomalhaut is referring to "what our students bring into our classes, from their attitudes, moods, and emotions to their motivations, instincts, and habits. All of these factors play into what students need individually and collectively in order to learn." Because I teach many first-generation college students, I find this a fascinating perspective, as well as Fomalhaut's argument that "the way we learn a craft is a holistic process of continual development." Fomalhaut's essay suggests that writing teachers consider the "whole writer" and develop a learning, "practice space wherein students can develop better work habits and rituals around writing." Fomalhaut notes that studio methods might have applications for writing instructors, allowing us to help students acquire "certain work habits, mindsets, and dispositions." As I read Fomalhaut's essay, I consider how I might focus more on "whole-body learning" that would develop not only writing skills but my students' study, work, and life skills.

While Fomalhaut alludes to possible application of studio models in composition classes, similarly, Pamela Henney examines how methods from other disciplines may have application in writing instruction. In "Acting the Author," Henney views the first-year composition course and the process that new students experience in their development as academic writers through the lens of Konstantin Stanislavsky's acting theory. The title of the essay, "Acting the Author," emphasizes some of the parallels between Method Acting and Method Writing. For instance, perhaps, there is a "process a method actor goes through to create and present his character within the context of a play or film," and, likewise, a "process an expository writer (journalist to essayist) goes through to create and present himself as the author of his text." These processes share a theory of mimesis, as defined by Stanislavsky and Aristotle, which may help students empower themselves as they strive to learn new roles and academic language. Our student writers must, just as performers do, visualize, rehearse, practice, and perform their new roles in the academy, which requires adopting a new discourse style and an academic Self. Henney argues that some of the techniques used by actors may apply to the needs of first-year composition students: "Using similar visualization and other acting techniques, first-year-composition students could more readily envision themselves as academic writers." First-year composition and the process new writers experience as they try to learn academic writing skills may parallel the method acting process. As a new paradigm, method writing in the composition class could help students visualize, rehearse, perform, improvise, and even believe their roles as academic writers.

Borrowing from another discipline, Casie Fedukovich applies somatic pedagogies and Human Movement Studies (often used in dance instruction) to the composition arena. Fedukovich hopes to "encourage students to be more present . . . both physically and intellectually" so that we can have more space for metaphorical *dance* in the writing classroom. After reviewing scholarship on "the teaching and learning body in composition," Fedukovich examines how rhetorical instruction has moved away from its classical, more holistic training, which included focus on the body in oratory instruction, to a context that often privileges the exchange of texts and that makes "human bodies virtually absent." Fedukovich is not trying to "conflate training dancers with teaching writing, but there are similarities," an argument that she makes quite persuasively. Fedukovich describes what she calls a "move to somatic composition instruction," a pedagogy that may include methods like moving meditation and mentoring, textural directives, recognizing the influence of text on bodies, or emphasizing face-to-face communication; practices that encourage us to create "pedagogical room to dance" and new spaces for learning.

Finally, the chapter concludes with Christopher Garland's reflective piece, "Who Decides My Grade? Reflections on Team Teaching and Peer Mentoring in First-Year Composition." Garland shares the process of how team-teaching works in the writing classroom. He suggests that "the co-taught classroom enables different approaches to teaching first-year composition." Further, it "challenges students to adjust to a collective pedagogy and fosters a dynamic that [has] application" beyond the classroom. Garland argues that this format may be particularly beneficial for graduate students who lack teaching experience, allowing them to work with veteran writing teachers. For those of us who help other teachers learn to teach writing, team teaching may be the ideal transition for our graduate students and new teachers, helping them navigate the space between being the student and being the teacher, and, in turn, we might help the next generation of writing teachers develop of a love for teaching.

Work Cited

Shaughnessy, Mina P. "Diving In: An Introduction to Basic Writing." *The Writing Teacher's Sourcebook*, edited by Edward P. J. Corbett et al. Oxford University Press, 2000, pp. 94–99.

Chapter 8. Holistic Learning for Real-Life Writers: A Call for Affective Pedagogy in First-Year Composition

Rachel Anya Dearie Fomalhaut
BINGHAMTON UNIVERSITY

In recent years, much attention has been paid to the effects of virtual classrooms and the impact of technology on education. Many are concerned with the changes that online education seems to involve, but within those concerns, there seems to be only a vague consensus on what we are supposedly losing via the move to online. Perhaps the lack of clarity regarding what we might be losing in the move to online education stems from gaps in our shared understanding of what happens in our classrooms that is not strictly intellectual, but rather fully embodied. I propose that we, as teachers, more intentionally engage the affective spheres of our classrooms, whether traditional brick-and-mortar or online. I use the term *affective* here to encompass a range of considerations about what both we and our students bring into our classes, from attitudes, moods, and emotions to motivations, instincts, and habits. All of these factors play into what students need individually and collectively in order to learn. I intend to prompt us to become more mindful of the holistic and embodied way in which learning occurs because the way we learn any craft—whether the craft of painting or of writing and thinking as a sociologist—is a holistic process of continual development. In other words, writers and disciplinary practitioners do not become better in discrete stages, nor do we develop our skills *solely* by widening our vocabulary or discussing written works with others. The process of learning to write better, both within the broad academic sense and within the more focused and specific requirements of any particular discipline, is a holistic and gradual process, necessarily involving the slow development of habits as well as a deepening understanding of such wide-ranging concepts as the ethics of persuasion, the *feel* of wordiness, and the well-practiced sense that a paragraph is out of place.

Because craft learning is a holistic process, I find it beneficial to articulate the pedagogy of craft learning through the language of affect, which engages not only the cognitive but also the emotional and physical realms of learning. Following a recent *affective turn* in literary theory, wherein theorists increasingly focus their attention on the emotional and physical realms in which writing and reading operate, I apply a similar terminology and methodological approach to the realm of writing pedagogy. What I term *affective pedagogy*[1] is any teaching method founded upon a consideration of students as holistic, whole body learners who are undergoing a continual and gradual process of development as writers. One of the central premises of an affective pedagogical approach to both first-year college writing and writing across the curriculum is that a particular kind of learning (i.e. intuitive rather than transmissible learning) is the goal of any teacher who is trying to pass along something other than memorizable facts, numbers, dates, or even procedures. Composition scholar and instructor Robert Danberg thoughtfully addresses the idea of non-transmissible learning. In his work, "Rhetorical Thinking as Dispositional: An Analytical Framework for Teachers," Danberg rethinks rhetorical concepts (such as proper source use) within the framework of *dispositions* and habits that a student can take on over time. He summarizes Perkins, Jay, and Tishman's view of dispositions as a framework that "describes the practitioner's knowledge when wisdom, intuition and judgment are required along with technical facility and formal field or domain knowledge" (Danberg "Rhetorical Thinking . . . " 17–18). A *writer's* wisdom and *intuition* are not merely intellectual matters; rather, they are tools gained through a process of holistic (i.e. academic as well as personal) development over time.

Starting from the premise that a particular, and tricky, kind of learning is our goal as writing teachers, I argue that the process of becoming a better writer occurs not only through the intellectual but also through the emotional, physical, and even spiritual dimensions of our students' capacities as learners. Perhaps more to the point, if we understand student learning as resting upon a notion of cognitive intellect that is inextricably bound to the affective *realms* of bodies, emotions, moods, and attitudes, then the question of whether or not it is our job to teach life skills (i.e. skills that extend beyond our classes, or even beyond any classes) becomes moot. I propose that teaching college writing cannot be separate from mentoring, because we cannot easily separate our students' development as writers from our students' holistic and personal development. This approach draws upon both my own experiences as a writing across the curriculum teacher as well as recent educational and neuroscientific theories of learning. Here I will outline some of the reasoning in support of a consideration of the affective realm of learning in writing pedagogy as well as look at some models for moving towards an affective pedagogy in college writing courses, namely the art studio, the psychomotor skills class, and the *flipped* classroom.

The idea that learning, like effective mentoring, is a holistic process that involves the learner's affective system as well as intellectual ability, is supported by recent neurobiological research. Ed Nuhfer, Director of Faculty Development and professor of Geoscience at California State University, Channel Islands has been advocating for affective pedagogy for several years. Working with Professor Maria Costa from CSU Los Angeles, Nuhfer put together faculty preparation materials that emphasize the importance of understanding the biological changes that occur in our bodies as we learn—changes that in fact must occur in order for learning to take place. In their description of the neurobiological characteristics of learning, they explain:

> . . . repeated use of developed neural networks causes the brain
> to coat these particular networks in myelin. As a result, the elec-
> trochemical signals that pass through the networks to the arms
> and fingers . . . can flow stronger, faster, and produce greater
> focus. . . . Once the needed networks form and become myelin-
> ized, the brain no longer needs to devote the immense energy
> needed to build them. Our conscious mind then becomes avail-
> able for other things. ("The Psychomotor Domain . . . ")

In their materials, Nuhfer and Costa put forth the claim that "All learning involves building and stabilizing neural networks," thus emphasizing the inextricability of cognitive learning from the physical and other affective realms. I'll return to this later, but for now what I want to draw your attention to is the holistic and affective nature of learning any craft or skill.

Our job as writing teachers, and indeed the job of most teachers, is not merely the transmission of memorizable information, such as grammar rules. Although the lecture model for teaching college writing is largely out of favor today, some of its suppositions regarding the transmissibility of writing skills persist in some seminar style composition classrooms. One of those suppositions shows up commonly in the idea that consumption causes production, and subsequently in more class time spent reading and discussing model essays than in students actually doing the grunt work of writing. I argue for a shift away from the commonly accepted notion that what goes in as reading material and abstract principles will come out as writing, or what I like to call the *trickle down* theory of writing. I agree there is value in the practice of providing and assigning model essays and other college level reading material to students. Mimicry is certainly a vital part of learning any craft, and reading college-level texts offers students exposure to new strategies for using language.

However, it is important to remember that mimicry is always a whole-bodied, or affective, affair. In his essay, "Modeling a Writer's Identity: Reading and Imitation in the Writing Classroom," Robert Brooke offers an interesting argument on the subject of imitation in writing classrooms. He suggests that writers do not imitate other writing so much as they imitate other writers. According to Brooke's concept of imitation, in which "Imitation as a learning/teaching strategy . . . is more concerned with the *identity* of the writer than the form of the text," students need opportunities to imitate and embody the writer who is their teacher as well as the student writers who are their peer-colleagues (23, original italics). Robert Danberg offers another way to describe the dynamic of whole-person imitation when he says that one of the jobs of the writing teacher is to give your students permission to be like you ("Educating . . . "). In order to provide students with ample opportunities to imitate the whole person that a writer is, I propose we organize our classes as spaces where students are provided with the time, space, and structured activities necessary to practice being new kinds of writer-selves in the company of other whole writers. An important distinction I wish to draw here is the difference between modeling as mentoring, which is accomplished by providing opportunities for *whole-writer*—imitation, and providing model writing (e.g. model essays) for consumption.

A rather size-able obstacle to the teaching as mentoring model that I advocate for here is that the ever-increasing adjunctification of higher education in the U.S. threatens the ability of college students to see their teachers as mentors who it would be desirable to imitate. This obstacle to mentoring is a particular problem in college writing courses, since a large proportion of both FYC and WAC courses are staffed by adjunct faculty earning barely or less than a living wage. The lack of institutional respect, resources, and compensation awarded to adjunct teachers make us very poorly positioned to act as mentor figures to our students, who are unlikely to look up to and attempt to imitate adults receiving such ill treatment in society. As an adjunct professor myself, I cannot in good conscience advise any of my students to "Be like me." This does not mean that the mentor model of teaching is ineffective, only that it becomes less and less available to a majority of college teachers with each passing year due to the increasing adjunctification and corporatization of higher ed.

In another chapter of this section, Pamela Henney suggests that writing teachers would do well to view our students' learning processes along the same lines as Method acting training. Henney argues that learning to write within a fairly unfamiliar academic setting and learning to Method act both involve a similar kind of whole-bodied rehearsing. In the case of writing across the curriculum, a student is essentially required to rehearse a performance of a new and unfamiliar academic identity in order to eventually be able to embody that identity at will and with enough ease to make the performance come off as wholly convincing in their writing. Henney writes: "The representational Stanislavsky's Method trains actors to move from external mimicking to internal experiencing to foster believable, spontaneous, inventive, honest, ergo credible characters in performance." I would argue that one of the primary factors that allows the college writing student's movement "from external mimicking to internal experiencing" to take place is the presence of a real live mentor in the classroom (i.e. the teacher) to mimic, as well as the presence of peers who are rehearsing the same move, albeit using varying styles and arriving at different degrees of effectiveness.

When composition classes spend more time discussing readings or disseminating information than writing, we take time away from learning opportunities that are structured to help our students embody—and become enculturated to—new writing habits. What I am arguing for is a shift away from seminar style, discussion based composition courses to classes that devote more than half the time spent in the classroom to the actual, often painstaking work that students must undertake as writers, whether that work is writing, researching, reading and note-taking, outlining, revising, editing and proofreading, or collaborating with peers at various stages of the writing process.

The question then becomes, how do we effectively structure ample opportunities for affective learning through *whole writer* mimicry in our courses? One idea is to *flip* our courses inside out. Salman Khan, in a TEDTalk in Spring 2011, offers the concept of the *flipped classroom*, which is a way to structure class time so that students read, view, and even preliminarily discuss course materials (i.e. articles and books but also PowerPoint lectures and educational videos) at home and do their *homework* in class. Khan and other advocates for the flipped classroom argue that the internet and other modern technologies for the dissemination and discussion of information (e.g. Blackboard, streaming video, blogs, etc.) make it possible for today's students to get the individualized help they need to successfully handle obstacles—such as writer's block or misunderstanding what an assignment is asking them to do—during class time. Such help might come in the form of one-on-one clarification or feedback from a teacher/mentor, or in the form of hearing how several peer writers are tackling the same assignment in peer review. One concrete suggestion for how to flip a writing across the curriculum classroom is to structure at least one class period per week so that students have at least twenty minutes for quiet writing and/or research time (I allow students to use headphones if they find that noise helps them get to work), followed by another twenty minutes of free choice, during which time students can continue to write or work individually, put a call out for a peer review group, or ask the teacher for assistance. I agree with advocates for the flipped classroom that, by structuring the majority of class time as a space and time within which students are expected to *get to work* (Danberg), teachers can better respond to student questions, frustrations, and problems as they arise. By following Salman Khan's and others' ideas for the flipped classroom, we can provide ample structured practice space wherein students can develop better work habits and rituals around writing.

There is a joke by late comedian Mitch Hedberg that goes something like: "My smoking friends tell me I have no idea how hard it is to quit smoking. But they're wrong. I do know how hard it is to stop smoking. It's as hard as it is to start flossing." Substitute the words, "exercising" or "writing an essay" at the end of the joke, and many of us can relate to the sentiment, as well as to the difficulty many of our student's experience trying to establish positive writing and other study/work habits for themselves. Many students (and teachers!) have trouble *getting to work* (Danberg). And just as a coach requires her athletes to practice regularly and in manageable amounts, usually with peer athletes also in training, developing writers need structured and regular practice alongside peer and model writers in order to habituate themselves to the process of getting to work when writing is the work that needs to be done. I propose that getting to work in the classroom, over and over, will help to create and stabilize the neural networks necessary for the establishment and maintenance of a healthy writing practice out of the classroom. In other words, *doing* the acts of writing with structured support during class time is perhaps the single most important piece of help we can offer our students to habituate them, in their bodies and minds, to what *getting to work with writing* means.

To return to Henney's analogy to Method acting training, she argues that "It would ease the tension of appropriating academic discourse if FYC students could envision themselves playing the role of the author or writer—and if we as academics could envision students' role playing as rehearsal for an eventual embodied performance within their academic writing." When I imagine a Method acting student rehearsing their role, I imagine that rehearsal happening both alone at home *and* in the classroom, in front of teachers and colleagues. If it is important for us to envision our students in "rehearsal for an eventual embodied performance within their academic writing," and I believe Henney's analogy to be right on, then we must set aside a large chunk of our weekly class time for students to rehearse their new roles as academic writers and thinkers—both within and across particular disciplines—in the presence of and in company with their mentor (i.e. the teacher) and their colleagues (i.e. their classmates). Setting aside a large portion of overall class time for students to rehearse their new roles takes away enough of the sting of insecurity that comes with that kind of identity rehearsal to allow the embodied performance to come more fully to fruition.

Perhaps the neediest population for affective pedagogy is first-year community college students, which is a diverse population of writers who in many cases are not only becoming acculturated to college but also to the particular rhythms and demands of a student lifestyle more generally. Many first-year community college students are returning to school after years, and, like their peers at four year schools, many bring ineffectual or poorly developed study skills and getting-to-work habits to their writing and other classes. In an informal interview with me, Professor Bruce Need, a veteran and highly respected English teacher at Tompkins Cortland Community College in upstate New York, suggested that because of the particular needs that many community college students present, one of our most important jobs as teachers is to provide them with opportunities to get habituated to working with us, i.e. with a professor/teacher figure, to being in a classroom with classmates, to producing school work on a regular basis: in essence, to being and working in a school setting.

There are other models besides the flipped classroom to look at when considering ways of incorporating affective pedagogies that focus on whole-body learning. For example, there are rich lessons to be learned from psychomotor pedagogies, as noted by Casie Fedukovich in another essay in this volume. Yoga, martial arts, and other exercise and sport classes offer writing teachers different ways to think about how to structure learning experiences with a consideration of the affective (i.e. physical and emotional) needs of learners in mind. Scholars Nuhfer and Costa encourage teachers to look to areas of psychomotor learning, such as learning to drive a car, to reflect on their own teaching practices. They write, "The transition from beginning awkwardly to gaining control comes *only* from creating and stabilizing the necessary neural networks through practice . . .

[the] responsibility of a teacher is to show the student how to practice effectively. . . . Only informed practice can produce mastery" (original italics). Nuhfer and Costa nudge teachers to reflect on what kind of structured practice our students need to create and myelinize the neural pathways required for the kind of writing they will be asked to do across and within academic disciplines. As we reflect, we do well to keep in mind the affective rituals and habits that have grown to surround and stabilize our own writing practices (e.g. eating certain snacks at scheduled break times, sitting in a favorite chair, free writing for three minutes before diving into any project) just as a yoga teacher might model her own rituals (e.g. stretching certain muscles before beginning, or meditating a certain amount of time at the end of each session) for her students to adopt.

A third model for a composition course that embraces affective pedagogy is the art studio classroom model. Robert Danberg, in his seminar on "Teaching the Writer's Imagination: How Can Creativity Be Taught?" proposes a consideration of any type of writing as a skillful art or craft that can be taught as other arts are taught. Danberg applies some of the core tenets, dynamics, and pedagogies that are foundational to studio art classes, and especially as they are articulated by the Harvard Zero Project, to college writing classes because he believes that both FYC and WAC courses are after a similar kind of learning. One major facet of studio classes that Danberg points out is that they tend to place more focus on doing the craft than on discussing the craft during class time. Similarly, the greater use of classroom time for writing—and researching, and editing, and collaborating— is one important feature of the affective pedagogy I describe.

Danberg's work on the application of the studio model to composition classrooms draws on a compelling study published in 2007 by the Harvard Zero Project. That study, titled "Studio Thinking," provides an in-depth articulation and explanation of the fact that the primary goal of any studio classroom, alongside the acquisition of concrete skills and techniques, is the attainment and sustenance of certain work habits, mindsets, and dispositions in its students. An important outcome of a studio-modeled college writing course, therefore, is that students learn more than how to work the tools and craft of writing. In a studio classroom, students also become aware, through reflective exercises and sharing their processes with one another, of how to consciously structure a work process for themselves. In other words, students learn how to *get to work* not only on the specific craft focused on in one studio classroom but also in other areas of their life where they want to hone their skills and knowledge.

One possible obstacle to a serious consideration of affective pedagogy is a perception that when we attempt to articulate our ideas about the affective realm, as Danberg puts it, "the ground gets soft" (Danberg "Rhetorical Thinking . . . " 143). A serious consideration of the affective realm and its ultimate inextricability from what many people think of as 'solitary cognition' relies upon an epistemology that has not been widely recognized nor granted much authority in our mainstream culture. The knowledge held by the emotional and physical (i.e. affective) experiences of our bodies is often not viewed as knowledge at all. But Catherine Lutz, in her anthropological study, *Unnatural Emotions*, articulates something of great relevance to educators and students when she writes that "[emotion] retains value as a way of orienting us toward things that matter rather than things that simply make sense" (5). In other words, emotion is the ultimate arbiter of meaning and value. Expanding on Lutz's ideas, I am interested in granting greater value and authority to different kinds of knowledge, such as, for example, emotionally informed knowledge and intuition.

In their article, "Intuition as Authoritative Knowledge in Midwifery and Homebirth," anthropologists Robbie Davis-Floyd and Elizabeth Davis ask why and how intuition as a mode of knowledge has become so devalued in American culture. Their study explores "the phenomenon of midwives' occasional willingness to rely on intuition as a primary source of authoritative knowledge." The authors use the midwifery model of intuition as authoritative knowledge to call for a change in the way mainstream culture conceives of knowledge and the authority that accompanies it (260). I find no coincidence in the fact that midwifery, a female-dominated if not entirely female populated profession and one that is perhaps the most firmly rooted in female traditions, offers one of the most salient examples of a consideration of intuition as authoritative knowledge. It is important to note that accusations of being "touchy feely" and caring too much about our students' lives are rooted at least partly in a patriarchal value system that simultaneously undervalues and genders as female the supposedly separate realm of emotions. Creator and Executive Editor of *The National Teaching and Learning Forum*, James Rhem, writes that considerations of affect in teaching has long been an arena of research that no faculty "want[ed] to touch . . . [because] Caring was *soft*. Learning was *critical, tough, hard*. Caring was, sad to say, *unmanly*, and thus not intellectual" (2). In unveiling the sexist underpinnings of our long-held avoidance of affective issues in education, we make ourselves more open to receiving and using long-held wisdom as well as recent research on learning.

Some may argue that a focus on the supposedly private and subjective experience of our bodies and emotions in the classroom prompts a turn away from the social and ethical matters so heavily emphasized by critique-focused, *post-process* seminar and discussion models for composition courses. However, it is important to remember that anthropologist Catherine Lutz and other scholars imagine emotions as foundationally social, Lutz writing that "Talk about emotions is simultaneously talk about society," due to the cultural construction of emotions and their inextricability from matters of politics, kinship, and community (6). Rather than prompt us to turn away from social and ethical *things that matter* to focus on supposedly private experiences of ourselves as affective and interiorized individuals, the affective pedagogy that I propose offers us richer opportunities to engage with and respond to the individual needs and motivations of our diverse student bodies. A turn towards affective pedagogy can serve to reframe recent concerns about the move to distance learning and help us create more conducive learning environments. I echo the calls by Rhem, Nuhfer, and Costa, as well as the call of many teachers and scholars in recent years, as I urge us to explore how we as teachers might more intentionally approach the affective spheres of our courses in order to more effectively engage our students' abilities and motivations to learn.

Note

1. It is important to note that the affective pedagogy I will describe and explore in this article differs from those pedagogies of the same name that enjoyed some popularity in the United States during the 1970's. Pedagogies termed "affective" in the 1970's most likely would be termed "therapeutic" in academic circles today. What I term "affective pedagogy" is not synonymous with what is currently termed "therapeutic education."

Works Cited

Brooke, Robert. "Modeling a Writer's Identity: Reading and Imitation in the Writing Classroom." *College Composition and Communication,* vol. 39, no. 1, February 1988, pp. 23–41.

Danberg, Robert. "Educating the Writer's Imagination: How Can Creativity Be Taught?" Binghamton University, Spring 2011, Graduate Seminar.

———. "Rhetorical Thinking as Dispositional: An Analytical Framework for Teachers." Dissertation, Syracuse University, 2010.

Davis-Floyd, et al. "Intuition as Authoritative Knowledge in Midwifery and Homebirth." *Medical Anthropology Quarterly,* vol. 10, no. 2, June 1996, pp. 237–269.

Khan, Salman. "Salman Khan: Let's Use Video to Reinvent Education." TEDTalks, March 2011. www.ted.com.

Lutz, Catherine. *Unnatural Emotions: Everyday Sentiments on a Micronesian Atoll & Their Challenge to Western Theory.* University of Chicago Press, 1988.

Need, Bruce. Personal Interview. 10 October 2012.

Nuhfer, Ed, and Maria Costa. "Psychomotor Domain—How We Learn Physical Skills Can Teach Us Something." *Support for Effective Teaching (OSET),* University of New Mexico. www.unm.edu.

Rhem, James. "The Affect Issue." *National Teaching and Learning Forum,* vol. 17, no. 2, February 2008, pp. 1–3.

Chapter 9. Acting the Author

Pamela Henney
KENT STATE

First-Year Composition (FYC) often begins with students and instructors alike maneuvering a field of expectations and fears. We hope students are well prepared but increasingly research is telling us something different. According to the National Public Policy and Higher Education, 60 percent of students entering four-year and two-year colleges or universities each year across the U.S. are unprepared or underprepared (*Beyond*). They are transitioning from a familiar world—where they are at once confident in their ability to learn, but unconfident with the many new expectations, and/or complacently satisfied their pre-college level writing abilities will suffice in this not-so-familiar world of varying discourses within the university. Although they bring a range of intellectual and emotional skills with them (see Fomalhaut), we easily recognize transitioning students as they attempt to write academically, only to misuse vocabulary, overuse punctuation, awkwardly phrase opinions, and illogically organize their presentations. In "Inventing the University," David Bartholomae explains:

> Every time a student sits down to write for us, he has to invent the university for the occasion—invent the university, that is, or a branch of it, like history or anthropology or economics or English. The student has to learn to speak our language, to speak as we do, to try on the peculiar ways of knowing, selecting, evaluating, reporting, concluding, and arguing that define the discourse of our community. (605)

The students are taking on new roles, and studying under new directors, but misrepresenting the academic roles they are attempting to play. They cannot help it; they have been trained to write externally—or even resist joining in conversations. Bartholomae is correct: "[Students] must dare to speak it or to carry off the bluff, since speaking and writing will most certainly be required long before the skill is acquired" (Bartholomae *Inventing* 606). It is a remarkable performance, which writing requires, and *mimesis,* which literally denotes imitation, but which in the acting theory of Konstantin Stanislavsky equates to a greater depth. Where a representational theatrical performance can be flat and superficial, a *mimetic* performance is a holistic transformation or morphing of an actor who seems to disappear, leaving only the fully embodied character in performance (Stanislavsky 26–27). A presentation of the Self of a character functions within its reality—all naturalness implied. This reflects an Aristotelian paradigm that remains a standard (though a contested standard) throughout the centuries. Aristotle approaches *mimesis* differently:

> Drama is usually conceived in Aristotelian terms, as a mimetic art distinguished by its manner of presentation (dramatic dialogue) and analyzable in terms of the object of its imitation (praxis action) and its constituent parts: mythos (plot), ethos (character), dianoia (thought), lexis (diction), melos (song), and opsis (spectacle). (Vince 41)

Aristotle's definition of *mimesis* is a synthesis of aspects of imitation. Similarly, Stanislavsky's Method Acting, in its organic definition, is a unique process which makes use of the influences and experiences we have in forming ourselves. The process parallels that which an actor goes through to create and present his character within the context of a play or film, and the process an expository writer (journalist to essayist) goes through to create and present himself as the author of his text (see also Fedukovich's "somatic composition").

We all mull things over and come to a discussion again and again with new insight, a new approach to the argument, or a new interpretation of earlier discussions (Fomalhaut). In this way, the writer creates and continually refines his character as he presents his case on paper. Ergo, the writer *rehearses,* according to Donald Murray in *Writing Before Writing*, writers experience as much pressure to *not* write as they do *to* write. Writing, he argues, "is best described by the word 'rehearsal' . . . writers are 'in a state of rehearsal all the time'" (376). Students, like actors, arrive at the university recognizing their new roles within new companies, bringing to those roles personal experiences, individual plans, and private dreams. Academia awkwardly supports that. We ask students to recreate themselves as academics—characters new and often unfamiliar. We require students to discuss their ideas on our terms, not theirs, using our language within our discourse. We expect assimilation as we evaluate their academic performance. Assimilation at times requires a façade—even if only temporary. FYC students believe themselves to be assimilated but their inexperience reveals the façade (Fomalhaut). Empowerment is the key to developing one's personal agency as the academic, Thomas Newkirk argues in *The Presentation of Self*. Further, students, like academics, also need to recognize the fact that the Self we are empowering has numerous constraints rather than autonomy (Newkirk 45). These constraints are played out daily before a variety of audiences. In the Erving Goffman sense, we are all always performing. But, as playwright Luigi Pirandello writes:

> Do we really see ourselves in our true and genuine reality, as we are, or don't we rather see ourselves as we would wish to be? Through a spontaneous inner artifice, the fruit of secret tendencies or of unconscious imitation, do we not in good faith believe we are different from what we substantially are? And we think, work, and live according to this fictitious yet sincere interpretation of ourselves. (transl. in Casey 51)

Who we are at any given moment may not be who we truly are, but it may yet be an honest vision. We visualize our roles and actions as we embody those roles, in a way using them as rhetorical moves to accomplish or enhance a specific interactive mission (Fomalhaut). Using similar visualization and other acting techniques, FYC students could more readily envision themselves as academic writers.

Creation of the author's character and audience are often discussed in relation to personal growth or to developing relationships, which can be a positive necessity and a cautionary lesson. In fact, "According to Quntilian (sic) the rhetorician must 'possess, *and be regarded as possessing*, genuine wisdom and excellence of character'" (qtd. in Newkirk 5). However, this relational development is rarely discussed as an essential piece of the academic writing process we encourage our students to utilize. The Method Acting process to holistically create and perform a believable character illuminates in some important ways the process a first-year college student, or even a high school student, goes through to develop a concept of himself as an author, as a writer, as well as a concept of himself in those roles relating to an audience (Fomalhaut). He outlines them in *An Actor's Work*, which is the diary of acting student Konstanin Nazvanov's two years of lessons under Arkady Tortsov. Both Nazvanov and Tortsov are alter egos of Stanislavsky reflecting his own actor training and teaching experience. The similarities between these developmental processes suggest the possibility of new pedagogical approaches to writing instruction which draw specifically from the teaching and practice of acting. Specifically, Stanislavsky's *Experiencing*, year one of training, provides those tools and specified practice for actors negotiating the aporia—space of doubt and simulated truth—between mimicry, or representation, and an authentic performance, or the embodiment of a character. Similarly, Stanislavsky's second year of study, titled *Empowerment,* offers exercises which can empower FYC students to negotiate with more confidence, inner strength, and more successfully critically construct their discursive identities.

Considering FYC writing as performance challenges the academy's boundaries (Fedukovich). Doing so highlights the intersections between various theories, bringing insight into issues of writing anxiety, concentration, motivation, etc. Knowledge of one's academic character may be created and disseminated offstage while drawing from a menagerie of influences and experience. Finally, one embodies that specific academic character through a recursive rehearsal process. The relationship between the somatic and the semiotic—the material world and textual meaning—is key. Language does not merely describe; it is a means to action. "All language is performative," Reed Way Dasenbrock writes in "J.L. Austin and the Articulation of a New Rhetoric. "In making an utterance, one performs an act, or—as Austin went on to say—a number of different acts simultaneously" (295). The application of this theory directly to writing may be better explained through the work of master writer and performer Mark Twain. In *Acting Naturally*, Randall Knoper observes that Mark Twain once critiqued a written version of the speeches of Robert Ingersoll, responding in a letter to the orator: "I wish I could hear you speak these splendid chapters before a great audience—to read them by myself and hear the boom of the applause only in the ear of my imagination leaves something wanting—and there is also a still greater lack, your manner, and voice, and presence" (116). Considering writing as a performance focuses the writer on the life of the words on the page. Performative theory offers the possibility for more and multiple analysis factors in studying the orientation and impact of textual discourse—written or oral—on an audience. Knoper's study extends Twain's position, arguing that the writing experience should be akin to a physical performance:

> These examples must suffice for the moment to support my point—that for Twain there existed a gestural, bodily dimension to words, and that this dimension helped credit utterances with a degree of immediacy inasmuch as they were automatic and unconscious. In Mark Twain's thinking, especially of the 1880s and 1890s, the gaps of representation might be bridged by linking thought and word, emotion and language, through physical mediums; a problem of realism and reference had a possible solution in this more direct concrete connection. (117)

Knoper describes the physical or bodily connection to writing in Darwinian terms (see also Fomalhaut; Fedukovich). Basically, the human mind responds equally whether an emotion, for example, is elicited in an actual event or a simulated one (88). Dasenbrock explains Austin's view of discourse: "All discourse is multifunctional, oriented both towards its subject and its audience" (298). This depth of coherence between the Self and words on the page only reinforces the *stage fright* of many FYC students. Despite the social construction of the Self, expressing any aspect of that Self on paper requires a very intimate engagement with a subject and an audience, even in academic discourse. Consider how often those of us who have already successfully appropriated the discourse become defensive when our own writing is challenged. How many argument responses have we publicly voiced or read in the so-called composition theory wars? It would ease the tension of appropriating academic discourse if FYC students could envision themselves playing the role of the author or writer—and if we as academics could envision students' role playing as rehearsal for an eventual embodied performance within their academic writing. In "Fear, Teaching Composition, and Students' Discursive Choices," Sally Chandler reminds us: "While identity conflicts are highly personal and remain enmeshed in individual psychology and identity development, this uniqueness does not preclude the possibility that anxiety might influence students to express those conflicts in predictable ways" (60). Still, for some FYC students, writing anxiety is so great that they illogically ask for fewer writing assignments, even though they recognize the course is focused on writing.

Generally, students see no distinction between Author and Writer. To them, a Writer records, summarizes, notes, argues, or explains ideas on paper and an Author is a Writer who is published or who gets paid (Fomalhaut). In fact, Foucault makes a clear distinction between these personas. He argues that the Author is historically situated with the text and bears legal ownership of the work, while the Writer, however, "is born simultaneously with the text, [and] is in no way equipped with a being preceding or exceeding the writing" (Foucault *Barthes* 5). The Writer has no history or experience. The Writer is present only during the performance and is gone, while the Author remains and is responsible for the writing. In this frame, students would agree writers are scribes; authors create—and they are neither. Joy Ritchie, author of "Beginning Writers: Diverse Voices and Individual Identity," however, frames the writer this way:

> When the writing class focuses on language as a productive, generative force for creating meaning and when it provides multiple audience responses to writing, it gives the beginning writer an opportunity to develop new ideas and new forms of writing, but it also allows her to try on new identities through the writing process. (Ritchie 155)

Likewise, Barbara Tomlison, author of "Characters as Coauthors," does not distinguish between author and writer arguing "Such metaphorical stories are an important means by which people understand their composing experiences only partly monitored, partly remembered, partly reconstructed" (422). All writers use their own stories—fully or in part—fed by their own experiences or histories as a means of describing their own writing processes. It is often argued that fictional characters actually write themselves into a work, so why not expository writers? Why not FYC students? Writing oneself into a work—fiction or expository—is wholly an act of engagement.

Method Writing in the FYC classroom would focus on experiencing academia and the academic role before eventually embodying or appropriating that role. Both experience and embodiment require multiple forms of improvisation and rehearsal—physically, as well as dialogically, and dialectically (see Fedukovich). Murray actually ties improvisation and rehearsal directly to the writing process, calling procrastination in writing *rehearsal*. He writes, "Rehearsal usually begins with an unwritten dialogue within the writer's mind. . . . The writer thinks about characters or arguments, about plot or structure, about words and line" (376). This dialogue takes the forms of note-taking, journaling, outlining, discussions, research, and sketches. "In the final rehearsal," Murray continues, "The writer produces test drafts, written or unwritten" (377). Stanislavsky's alter ego Nazvanov began his acting courses by preparing dramatic scenes for performance with his assigned group, requiring discussions of scene options and casting their roles based on skill levels. Research was also required into not only the plays and roles, but also the acting notes and recalled performances of famous actors and acting coaches. Nazvanov admits he stopped reading the script early on, convinced that he knew his assigned character, therefore slacking in preparation and rehearsal. On day three, he decides he's ready to rehearse before his classmates, who negatively critique his work. Nazvanov's experiences are similar to FYC students in their first few days of writing class in that they frequently fall back on what is familiar, writing as they have for previous, non-university courses. Nazvanov, however, has the benefit of Tortsov's lessons—or Stanislavsky's Method. In his introduction, Stanislavsky explains the Method is not only for use in acting. Acting is only the frame Stanislavsky uses in discussing creativity: "So actors and others working in the theatre should create *who* and *how* they please but on one essential condition: that their creative process should not run counter to nature and her laws" (xxviii). The nature of the character being embodied and performed is already known by all who have read the play and the author's other works. This utilization of both internal and external experiences and observations in the Method might become a tool for resolving the theoretical and pedagogical differences in understanding FYC students and their development in the academy through writing.

Acting requires believability within false circumstances. The actor cannot change that role or the familiarity of it; he must present it entirely as the author intended. The actor must adapt, making the audience and fellow characters on stage believe he is who the character says he is—despite the actor's possible real life lack of experience. Acting is not mere external representation of a stereotype. Stanislavsky explains through Tortsov:

> Everything onstage must be convincing for the actor himself, for his fellow actors and for the audience. Everything should inspire belief in the possible existence in real life of feelings analogous to the actor's own. Every moment onstage must be endorsed by belief in the truth of the feelings being experienced and in the truth of the action taking place. (154)

Similarly, composition students are required to display this believability. If a student chooses to argue academically against civil disobedience, the reader expects the student to provide relevant illustrations of non-violent protests and provide research of negotiation techniques. This is what an academic does, and the reader must believe the student is an academic—despite the student's lack of experience as such. These are performances for the actor and the student—performances which require experiences they do not yet have or have not yet internalized. It is human nature to be comfortable with an external representation of an experience, but it takes practice to internalize an experience. The representational Stanislavsky's Method trains actors to move from external mimicking to internal experiencing to foster believable, spontaneous, inventive, honest, ergo credible characters in performance:

What does it mean to play 'credibly?' Nazvanov asked Tortsov, his acting instructor. "That means thinking, wanting, striving, behaving truthfully, in logical sequence in a human way, within the character, and in complete parallel to it. As soon as the actor has done that, he will come close to the role and feel as one with it. . . . Our purpose is not to create 'the life of the human spirit in a role,' but also to communicate it outwardly in an artistic form. (Stanislavsky 19–20)

That happens, according to Stanislavsky, through a number of simultaneous activities which must be practiced *un*-simultaneously. In other words, to ensure a natural flow, one must make a series of actions appear to be unrehearsed by not practicing each move in order. Consider how one moves across the room. Onstage perhaps one is not meant to be noticed as he moves across the room, or perhaps he is meant to hold the focus of the audience, blinding them to what else may be happening on stage. Breaking up entire series of action into skills makes it appear to be like any familiar skill and drill approach, but it is not. This is rehearsal: the type of rehearsal that Murray noted is necessary. The exercises are preparation during rehearsal, but each exercise is evaluated individually and immediately—a self-evaluation, a peer evaluation, an instructor and/or a director evaluation. Note: No audience evaluation is yet considered. This is practice discovering and experiencing. Only later do those skills play a part in fostering the creation and embodiment of a character performance before an audience. As the character focuses on his task onstage, the audience follows that intense focus. The actor embodying the character refocuses the audience's observation of the action. Embodying a character requires negotiation. Despite one's doubts, one must negotiate the character's construction in one's own terms, before finally embodying or, to use Bartholomae's terms, *appropriating*, the character. However, as noted earlier, one often gives in to the doubt, clinging to one successfully negotiated and powerful aspect of the character and ignoring all the others.

In Stanislavsky's terms, such negotiation *is* embodiment: "You must absorb and filter any system through yourself, make it your own, retain its essentials and develop it in your own way" (Stanslavsky xxv). In *Embodiment*, Stanislavsky offers exercises targeting basic underlying or building block skills, similar to those offered in *Experiencing*. These are not meant to help the actor create the character, but to *refine* the character which is already created. This natural appearance is what Bartholomae is concerned about when he allows that students must "carry off the bluff" (605). Through Method acting's character development techniques, FYC students should not only perform more authentically and naturally when acting the academic role and acting the author role, but they may also begin *embodying* their roles on stage—or on paper. In fact, the Self is informed as much by the character developed for performance, as the character is informed by the Self. The key is control—and polish, or *finish* as Stanislavsky calls it: "The more control and finish acting has, the calmer the actor is, the more clearly the shape and form of the character comes across and the more it affects the audience and the greater success the actor has" (543). Likewise, the First-Year Composition student.

Works Cited

Barthes, Roland. "The Death of the Author." *The Death and Resurrection of the Author?*, edited by William Irwin. Greenwood Press, 2002, pp. 3–8.

Bartholomae, David. "Inventing the University." *The Norton Book of Compositional Studies*, edited by Susan Miller. W.W. Norton & Co., 2009, pp. 605–630.

———. "Writing Assignments: Where Writing Begins." *Writing on the Margins: Essays on Composition and Teaching.* Bedford/St. Martin's, 2004, pp. 177–191.

"Beyond the Rhetoric: Improving College Readiness Through Coherent State Policy." The National Center for Public Policy and Higher Education, 2010.

Casey, Mary. "Building a Character: Pirandello and Stanislavsky." *Luigi Pirandello: The Theatre of Paradox.* Edwin Mellen Press, 1996, pp. 50–65.

Chandler, Sally. "Fear, Teaching Composition, and Students' Discursive Choices: Re-Thinking Connections Between Emotions and College Student Writing." *Composition Studies*, vol. 35, no. 2, Fall 2007. *Academic Search Complete*, pp. 53–70.

Dasenbrock, Reed Way. "Truth and Methods." *College English*, vol. 57, no. 5, September 1995, pp. 546–561.

Foucault, Michel. "What is an Author?" *The Death and Resurrection of the Author*, edited by William Irwin. Greenwood Press, 2002, pp. 9–22.

———. "Writing the Self." *Foucault and His Interlocutors*, edited by Arnold Davidson. University of Chicago Press, 1997, pp. 234–247.

Henney, Pamela. *Acting the Author/Writer: Using Acting Techniques in Teaching First Year Composition.* Master's thesis, University of Akron, 2012.

Knoper, Randall. *Acting Naturally: Mark Twain in the Culture of Performance.* University of California Press, 1995.

Murray, Donald. "Writing Before Writing." *College Composition and Communication*, vol. 29, no. 4, December 1978, pp. 375–381.

Newkirk, Thomas. *The Performance of Self in Student Writing.* Boyton/Cook, 1997.

Ritchie, Joy. "Beginning Writers: Diverse Voices and Individual Identity." *College Composition and Communication,* vol. 40, no. 2, 9 May 1989, pp. 152–174.

Stanislavsky, Konstantin. *An Actor's Work: A Student's Diary*, edited and translated by Jean Benedetti. Routledge, 2008.

Tomlison, Barbara. "Characters are Coauthors: Segmenting the Self, Integrating the Composing Process." *Written Communication*, October 1986, pp. 421–448.

Vince, Ronald. "The Aristotelian Theatrical Paradigm as Cultural-Historical Construct." *Theatre Research International*, vol. 22, no. 1, 1997, pp. 38–47.

Chapter 10. Free to Dance: A Somatic Approach to Teaching Writing

Casie J. Fedukovich
NORTH CAROLINA STATE UNIVERSITY

"Beyond the realm of critical thought, it is equally crucial that we learn to enter the classroom 'whole' and not as 'disembodied spirits.'"

—*bell hooks, Teaching to Transgress*

The Return-and-Dash

Graded papers in a stack, students lined up like they're waiting at the DMV or the health center. I work to give neutral face. On this day in November, the heating in our classroom had been preemptively triggered by a week of unseasonable cold. The return to late-summer temperatures made it at least 85 degrees inside. On this day, I should have followed experience and chosen the cardigan. My white button down grew ever more transparent.

The Return-and-Dash is always awkward, made that way by the process of assessment. On this day in November, it's made more awkward by my hyperawareness of temperature and my body. *Please just take them and go*, I think. And their responses satisfy: silently flip to the back page, scan for the grade, and leave.

The practice is largely unsatisfying to all involved. Student: Here's my text, a proxy for my thoughts. Teacher: Here's my text alongside, marginalia-cum-thought. See me if you have questions. Know this: If you do have questions, they will be coded as lack of understanding, disengagement from process, or resistance to assessment. (Students are taught that it's better *not* to have questions.) On this day in November, the complex exchange is further framed at the moment when I'm feeling like my skin might melt, and I'm half-crazy with anxiety as to what other corporeal shapes are becoming more noticeable in the heat.

In many of our writing classrooms, it may seem that bodies become salient only when they cause problems, need remediation, or fit imperfectly into our planned pedagogies, most of which privilege clear and confident prose as the most valuable exchange we can make with students. This chapter presents the idea of somatic—or body-centered—pedagogies by connecting the writing classroom with Human Movement Studies. Such "embodied literacies" (Kerkham, Fleckenstein) provide an opportunity to think about text as beyond the alphabetic. As Kristie Fleckenstein notes, "[T]ext refers not only to textbooks but also to any artifact that might help us attend to the edges that blur," including corporeal ones (105). My students on that warm November day may have been reading my marginal and terminal comments as authoritative and punitive. I was concerned they would read my body counter to that authority. In this case, the text to be read extended beyond the page to include the performance of handing back papers in an educational setting, a routine made more complicated by factors like the heat and my affective context.

If embodied literacies help us revise and extend the meaning of *text* to include non-alphabetic artifacts, even dynamic artifacts like bodies, we consequently are open to revising concepts like *Writing* and *Curriculum*. Compositionists often frame Writing Across the Curriculum (WAC) as a vertical model that distributes alphabetic (printed) writing throughout a student's college experience, starting with first-year composition. However, we may productively borrow methods and epistemologies from other fields—in this case, Human Movement Studies with a focus on dance—to enrich our teaching of writing and rethink our definitions of text, writing, and curriculum. In proposing a more interdisciplinary model for writing studies, I am not advocating Writing in the Disciplines (WID), though this curriculum may be used. Instead of exploring how other disciplines conduct research or share their findings, an interdisciplinary writing classroom would import pedagogies from other fields in order to meet the needs of our students and enliven our teaching.

The study and practice of rhetoric is historically grounded in a more holistic understanding of the body, but our first-year writing classrooms overwhelmingly privilege student texts—and teacher textual response—as the primary pedagogical tools. These practices—trading text for text—are informed by social expectations of higher education and metrics-based secondary schooling practices, in addition to shared disciplinary attitudes about teaching writing. (See Rachel Fomalhaut's piece in this collection, "Holistic Learning for Real-Life Writers," for a more in-depth treatment of the topic).

In this chapter, I wish to raise questions about our current educational context in the corporatized classroom—with its emphasis on metrics and top-down Common Core—to consider Patricia Cranton's statement: "It takes only a few minutes' thought to list a dozen characteristics of educational systems that seem deliberately designed to take the soul out of teaching and learning" (126). By reflecting on ways we can seek soul in teaching, by giving ourselves and our students room to dance, we can productively resist these dominant educational structures. What follows is an exploration of the concealed bodies in composition and suggestions for moving away from the primacy of the written to incorporate movement as a composition pedagogy. The goal is to encourage students to be more present in our classrooms, both physically and intellectually. Further, and to illustrate the core purpose of this collection, a somatic pedagogy would center composition in individual student bodies to engage students in their own education, to make space for them to practice agency at a time when learning has been constructed as a passive act. Somatic pedagogies thus have the potential to radically influence how students perceive their own roles in education and, by extension, their power as informed citizens influenced by material culture.

Embodied Intelligence: The Move from Public Speaking to Private Management

Rhetoric's long history supplements composition's short one by more fully attending to the body-as-text, with discussions of the flesh most closely focused on codifying its rhetorical potential. For example, Greek methods of holistic training, detailed by Debra Hawhee as a process of "virtuosity inhered in corporeality," a process of "seeing and recognizing" a body's physical and intellectual potential (4). In addition, textbooks like Austin's *Chironomia*, a guide for the "proper regulation of the voice, the countenance, and the gesture," position the body as an integrated, trainable, and iterative mode of appeal. The Greek concept of *metis*, or the "mode of negotiating agonistic forces, the ability to cunningly and effectively maneuver a cutting instrument, a ship, a chariot, a body, on the spot, in the heat of the moment" (Hawhee 47), underpins this embodied intelligence. Care of the body supports cognition, and synthesis of the body with language becomes a crucial final step in a successful oration.

It stands to reason, then, that the move from apt oration to fluency with written text as the measure of a learned person shrinks delivery as it accentuates invention, arrangement, and style. The move gradually de-emphasized rhetoric as human interaction; instead, rhetoric—as it tends to be taught in our composition classrooms—engages unidirectional, non-specific utterances for generic layperson audiences (see Ong). Students have been trained against considering themselves part of the "Conversation of Mankind" (Bruffee), where rhetorical motivation and consequence are intimately tied to in-flesh audiences and the real-life consequences of rhetoric. The result: Our writing courses, situated as they are in the humanities, can make human bodies virtually absent.

Prior scholarship on the teaching and learning body in composition has been discussed under a number of rubrics: critical pedagogies, feminism, histories of rhetoric, disability studies, and critical race theory, to name only a few. Student bodies have been reduced to sites of cultural reproduction and schools to oppressive status-quo factories that use pedagogic authority as a "substitute for physical constraint" in order "to produce a permanent disposition to give, in every situation . . . , the right response" (Bourdieu 36; see also Bernstein; Bowles and Gintis; Giroux). Scholars such as Ira Shor and Henry Giroux have suggested how teachers and students alike may physically resist these spatial models of playing school. Shor's "Siberian" students, for example, populate the back row, and thus trouble the territory of the composition classroom by remaining physically present while cuing themselves as pedagogically absent. In this way, Shor argues, they "appear to both reject authority and submit to it at the same time" by positioning themselves as far away from the teacher's podium as the space allows (12). Their bodies provide the vehicle for this quiet act of resistance.

More recently, theorists have posited teacher-body-as-text via identity categories like race, gender, class, and sexuality (Kopelson; hooks; Kirsch et. al). Kopelson warns against organizing under any managed identity, as students then read teachers reductively, to make what is partial whole and generalizable (23). The conclusion seems to be that students take up classroom scripts per their cultural training and that teachers' bodies—how they are coded, read, and enacted— become perhaps the most important texts in the class. Students read them as authority, sometimes as novel or superficially transgressive, and no measure of classroom decentering changes the fact of end-of-semester assessment. However, the interaction is never absolute: Moments of resistance to dominant educational models can happen. Even as the stage of the composition classroom is inscribed through layers of institutional power and social expectation, these boundaries can be playfully disrupted.

Somatic pedagogies, as I sketch them out, borrow ideas from Human Movement Studies, specifically dance, to recognize that even as our student and teacher populations become more diverse and as instructional methods innovate with new technologies, the old ways of trading text for text stand. Bodies in composition become salient only when they are disruptive or need accommodating; writing is our body's commodity in the composition classroom, both students' texts and teachers' marginalia. A move to incorporate somatic pedagogies can upset this overvaluation of textual product to emphasize processes that address felt needs and encourage presence.

The Anesthetized Classroom

The writing classroom often makes part of its goal recognition and analysis of aesthetic or pathetic features of texts. Our assessment practices, however, tend toward the anesthetic: at a remove, etymologically "without sensation" (OED). Our daily classroom practices may also reflect this deadening of sense.

Epistemologically, we know that students gain situated knowledge anchored in the body and that the negotiated truths of the composition classroom filter through sociopolitical histories, which can never be separated from the body. Realistically, the increasingly corporatized structure of the higher education system forces us to greater efficiency. Cranton notes, "[l]arge lumbering systems that see themselves as needing to be accountable to those who fund them . . . cannot be much bothered with the joy of learning" (126). She continues to argue that the very terms we use to describe our labor constrain how we think and perform it: lecturers lecture, teachers grade papers, students arrive to class prepared to passively accept instruction (Cranton 127; see also Horner).

Students and teachers alike operate within these practiced paradigms of acceptable school behavior. It is a deeply held tenant of schooling in America:

All physical action must be cleared with the teacher. To implement somatic pedagogies in first-year writing, then, is to ask students to question at least twelve years of bodily instruction. The composition course may thus encourage the very actions students have been trained to consider off-limits. The shift is no less than a move from rugged individualism—and solipsistic views of features like error—to recognition of socially negotiated truths. It's a move from training compliant employees to recognizing the creative power of many minds and bodies working together, a move that unravels students' taken-for-granted ideas about learning: how it happens, who it's for, and what it does. Matthew Heard, drawing from philosopher Carlos Sini's *The Ethics of Writing*, reframes writing as a "living habit of being" emphasizing responsiveness (42). This framework privileges the body as a locus of knowledge—and thus as an important consideration in praxis—to help move composition instruction into the realm of the somatic.

Defining Somatic Learning

I do not wish to conflate training dancers with teaching writing, but there are similarities. Most salient is the mutual connection to training a familiar responsiveness to kiarotic exigencies. Just as a dancer must know the next appropriate step or steps, a writer must be able to feel through the constraints and affordances of each discrete rhetorical situation to provide the most fitting response. Thomas Hannah's foundational definition of somatics encourages whole-person consideration: "Any viewpoint of the human being that fails to include both the first-person, somatic view and the third-person, physiological view is deceptive. To view a human only as a third-person, externalized body is to see only a physical puppet or dummy" (20). Somatic awareness or body-centered learning, according to Liora Bresler, implicates pedagogies that recognize that "[T]he body is personal. At the same time, it has a tremendous capacity to connect with others" (128). Bresler goes on to describe the choreography of the classroom: students raise hands, teachers direct bodies in prescribed paths. Everyone dances the dance of formalized education, and those out of step are recognized as disruptive.

Peggy Phelan, performance theorist, writes, "The body is always a disciplined entity. One part is temporal linguistic, the other is temporal physical" (qtd. in Ross 173). Here, she sketches the recursive path of student response, tied in writing classes to texts, as both creating and supporting practices that keep students physically, and perhaps intellectually, still. Compliant students and docile bodies are rewarded, echoing Bourdieu's definition of schooling. Janice Ross clarifies this dichotomy through a familiar student/prisoner metaphor, focusing on the dance class: "Sitting down is interdict, unless one is specifically told to do so. The bodies in this space are to be primed and alert, freed temporarily of appetites and bodily needs and prepped to explode into physical action" (169). Quick substitutions—standing up for sitting down, physical for textual—

move this landscape of the dance class to the writing class. Ross continues: "The body-of-knowledge becomes the body-of-means and the body-in-view" (169). In composition, students' texts efface their bodies-of-view, just as marginalia efface instructor bodies.

A move to somatic composition instruction undoes the way most students have participated in scenes of humanities education, as much of the learning expected of them is assumed to take place outside the classroom. Assessment of that learning, usually in the form of evaluation of polished prose, considers the final inscribed form as the best representation of the mind's work. Even as composition values writing processes, it is the final draft that instructors heavily weigh. Visible classroom engagement often takes the shape of collaboration and inventional work, methods used by many composition instructors. These managed practices are comfortable to both students and teachers, as they support prior training foregrounding teacher expertise and classroom control, where the teacher is the only body sanctioned to move freely about the room. However, radical pedagogies that begin to interrogate the foundations of how knowledge is created, assessed, and reinforced—and that begin to trouble our assumptions about teaching writing—indicate that physical movement and recognition of situated learning work together to promote engagement (Lave and Wenger).

A Somatic Class in Situated Practice

Knowing that student and instructor bodies are held to culturally reinforced roles, and that these roles tend to elide difference and enforce silence and stillness, how might a composition instructor encourage the body's potential?

Dance.

Dance textually, dance actually; take joy in teaching and in students' inquiry into their world. The following methods do not presume physical mobility by either instructor or student. As Petra Kuppers, a self-identified "disabled dance teacher" attests: "My goal in performance and choreography is to make bodies and spaces strange and interesting" (122). Her wheelchair holds the "potential for movement," and she trains her dance students to recognize her kinesphere, or personal space, as complex and responsive. We can thus disrupt the pathways that students have (usually grimly, usually passively) followed prior to their entry in our classes by recognizing the individual impact each of them make with their physical and intellectual presence.

What follows are a few methods I've used in my own classrooms to create these disruptions. They're influenced by the work of the performance theorists I've noted, as well as accepted disciplinary practices in composition. The list is partial and situated, and I've worked to address the issues of access that a discussion of movement necessarily implicates.

Moving Meditation and Mentoring

I recognize that moving mediation, per Thoreau, might present a prohibitive activity for some teachers and students. But the principle remains: Be removed from the bounds of the office or the classroom when possible. Take in the fresh air. If walking is comfortable, do so. Sitting and talking about writing in an office, with a text front-and-center, surrounded by books and to-do lists, reinforces the act of writing as only the textual representation of thought and as work. Stroll, broadly conceived, and ask students to narrate their thoughts as you do.

Standing and Sitting, Leaning, Lying Down

I once invited students to write in class in the way that was most comfortable for them, as long as they didn't impede anyone else's progress or create distress. Quite naturally, one student stretched out full length on the floor (with its dirty carpet and all). Opening the classroom space beyond the obligatory rows or falsely democratic circle (or even the assumption that we *sit in chairs to learn*) asks students to query their material needs when writing.

Muscle Memories

Offering students frequent impromptu opportunities for physical engagement—positioning themselves at the front of the class to present work, circulating the room, creating visually on whiteboards—reinforces the material concerns of writing and of kairotic responsiveness. Simple tools like multicolored sticky notes invite students to move about the room as they collaborate. We've charted arguments, outlined assignments, parsed rhetorical elements, and participated in ad hoc Post-It sessions, where students designed and presented analyses on large post-it notes.

Further, I try to disrupt the notion that speakers should address the class only when they are prepared to deliver a polished argument. Students too easily fall into operationalized hierarchies where only teachers and students-prepared-to-act-as-teachers are qualified to speak. Making presentation both routine and casual invites students to become more active learners while deemphasizing the importance of the one-shot-best-shot group presentation. This practice is initially met with resistance but, on reflection, students overwhelmingly evaluate it as useful in breaking down anxieties, getting comfortable with verbally presenting ideas, and building classroom community.

Textual Directives

Asking students to write textual directive, or steps, for their peers encourages them to consider the physical implications and assumptions of their texts. We've written instructions as simple as turning on a laptop and as complex as dance steps. Reflecting on taken-for-granted movements works to make the familiar strange.

Shifting Our Texts

That we move bodies in two ways, with physical force or with language, is one of the first, and perhaps most foundational, lessons students can learn from first-year composition, and it becomes one of the most important lessons they transfer into their other classes and careers. In this way, we reframe text as holding the potential for physical consequence. For example, presenting declarations of war as utterances that move physical bodies into conflict with other physical bodies illustrates the power of textual communication. I solicit course texts for analysis from students' lives, and they have been as varied as health insurance benefit guides, pre-natal care directives, gym memberships, and pancake preparation instructions.

Performing Our Research

Scripting and performing research stories encourages students to translate data between genres and practice meeting the expectations of different audiences. As a follow-up to a fieldworking paper, I asked students to script short monologues from the point of view of a composite character created from interview, survey, and observation data. Living the research story demands that these novice researchers practice reflexivity to question their presuppositions about the research scene and participants. The texts produced are in-flesh, drawn from living sources, as is the audience. When making these projects open to the public (usually a smattering of colleagues and a few students' friends) some monologues were met with standing ovations.

Contextualized and Individual Assessment

It is unrealistic expectation to conference with each student multiple times throughout the semester. I have managed to find a workable semi-solution by handing back papers individually in class while students collaborate. The scene of return is less private than an office; however, making eye contact and narrating my process assures students that I did, indeed, thoughtfully read their work, while also giving them the opportunity to ask questions or voice concerns. Because of time constraints, around five minutes for each conference, I follow a 1:2:2 schedule: one minute for my voice, two minutes for the student to skim the paper silently, two minutes for questions. Of course this structure is far from perfect—both parties feel rushed. But compared to the anxious steps of the Return-and-Dash, these brief conversations allow students to engage with the process as active partners. Of course, if students have in-depth questions about their grades—or I have to have a conversation with a student that demands attention to FERPA regulations—I will negotiate those needs individually.

Bodies Outside the Classroom

These methods are framed in terms of training responsiveness. Through repetition of movement—addressing the class as an expert, for example, or exploring ideas verbally, face-to-face—students begin to integrate more holistically the practices of thoughtful rhetors. These low-stakes opportunities in the first-year writing classroom can build habits that inform students' practices in college beyond first-year composition and in both personal and professional venues. I've offered four potential implications:

- Recognizing material needs and consequences: When we recognize materiality in our teaching practices, our students learn more about what they need to thoughtfully engage and confidently generate. Bodies are never without restraint: As students, teachers, and employees, we are each expected to fall in line with social norms. However, trying on new ways of learning and communicating—composing in different scenes, for example—may help students understand the material effects of work outside the academy and how they may revise their work practices to meet their personal needs. In this way, as students chart their future plans, they may have clearer ideas about what they need to flourish.
- Recognizing the influence of text on bodies: Our students are awash in communication, even as we fuss about how little they read and write. Much of their social interaction is textual, through quick messages on phones and social networks, but their engagement with these texts often remains passive. By reintroducing the physical consequences of real-world texts— laws, medical directives, work contracts, custody agreements, declarations of war—we help them critically and creatively tangle with the texts they'll encounter, and produce, throughout their lives.
- Emphasizing face-to-face communication: As more college courses choose to expand their offerings to include distance-education methods, in-person interaction in small classes has become rare. Our students, as a result, are getting fewer opportunities to practice professional oral communication and even casual conversation outside their peer groups. Somatic pedagogies, by reinforcing in-person rhetorical responsiveness, necessarily value face-to-face communication in low-stakes scenes by mixing registers and encouraging spontaneous conversations among teachers and students. The idea here is to move away from the sedimented relationships we feel constitute our role (and thus our students' roles) in the first-year writing classroom to include a greater valuation of the

casual and playful. In this way, we can help students—even in short interchanges—practice the conversation(s) of (hu)mankind.

- Training process: Finally, somatic pedagogies may help students learn more about their learning processes, specifically moving-to-learn and talking-to-learn analogous to writing-to-learn (WTL) strategies. By deemphasizing the written text as the most important measure of learning in the composition classroom, we revise practices to give greater weight to the cognitive processes that precede writing. This approach does not presume to answer questions of duality nor to excerpt writing from the writing classroom; it does, however, acknowledge that learning occurs dialogically and dialectically. Since many real-world situations expect on-the-fly, heat-of-the-moment responses, training students in process work can inform their professional identities by preparing them to interact in situations that call for immediacy. Having students, for example, routinely address the class before they've polished their ideas thus builds a storehouse of practices with direct professional parallels.

Making pedagogical room to dance—to engage with and create new scenes of learning—frees teachers and students from the clinch of top-down corporate delivery structures that have taken over many of our classrooms. Some of these structures may emerge as policy language in our individual writing programs. One doesn't have to look far to find programs where revision is discouraged (on the basis, perhaps, that it's unrealistic to get a second chance in a real-life setting) or where required page production overshadows student engagement in process. Teachers looking to incorporate somatic pedagogies in the context of administrative oversight may choose to explore flexible gray areas, places where policies do not prescribe action.[1]

Further, building in opportunities for students to practice presence, instead of acting at a remove where they passively accept knowledge, is to encourage them to value their experiences as meaningful educational engagement. This engagement may take the form of a dress rehearsal, as Pamela Henny notes, drawing from Konstantin Stanislavsky's ideas on method acting. It may also look like the holistic, affective pedagogies proposed by Rachel Anya Dearie Fomalhaut. These methods take into account "intuitive rather than transmissible learning," a sort of learning "by feel" keyed to individual student needs (17). If we offer students opportunities to practice the moves of academia off the page—as actors or dancers, over time, with regard to the complexity of their whole selves—we may help them build the fluency and confidence to control printed text, still a highly-valued commodity, while also encouraging creative, embodied ways of thinking.

These methods go beyond decentering the classroom. Students recognize the artificial democracy of circled desks and negotiated syllabi. A somatically-informed composition class honors students' lived experiences, their first-person selves as well as ours, while also reintroducing in-the-flesh audiences for classroom texts (Hannah 20). These methods may offer a counterpoint to the soulless bureaucracies that dog our composition pedagogies, encouraging both students and teachers to joyfully engage in the writing classroom. We show our students that learning must move beyond rote memorization and repetition to include their voices as the next generation of thinkers and doers.

Note

1. This chapter does not wish to ignore the material realities for those teaching in insecure positions, but it cannot give the situation the attention it requires here. Somatic pedagogies thus have ramifications for teachers and students alike, as they intersect with administrative oversight in some programs.

Works Cited

"Anaesthetic, n." The Oxford English Dictionary, 2nd ed. OED Online. Oxford University Press, 1 May 2012.

Austin, Gilbert. Chironomia. Bulmer and Company, 1806. Google Books.

Bernstein, Basil. Class, Codes, and Control, 3 vols., 1971. Routledge, 2008.

Bourdieu, Pierre. Outline of a Theory of Practice. Cambridge University Press, 1977.

Bowles, Samuel, and Herbert Gintis. Schooling in Capitalist America. Basic Books, 1976.

Bresler, Liora. "Dancing the Curriculum: Exploring the Body and Movement in Elementary Schools." Knowing Bodies, Moving Minds: Towards Embodied Teaching and Learning, edited by Liora Bresler. Kluwer, 2004, pp. 127–152.

Bruffee, Kenneth. "Collaboration and the 'Conversation of Mankind.'" College English, vol. 46, no. 7, 1984, pp. 635–652.

Cranton, Patricia. "The Resilience of Soul." Pedagogies of the Imagination: Mythopoetic Curriculum in Educational Practice, edited by Timothy Leonard and Peter Willis. Springer, 2008, pp. 125–138.

Fleckenstein, Kristie. Embodied Literacies: Imageword and a Poetics of Teaching. Southern Illinois University Press, 2003.

Giroux, Henry A. Theory and Resistance in Education. Heinemann Educational Books, 1983.

Hannah, Thomas. Somatics: Reawakening the Mind's Control of Movement, Flexibility, and Health. Addison Wesley, 1988.

Hawhee, Debra. Bodily Arts: Rhetoric and Athletics in Ancient Greece. University of Texas Press: 2005.

Heard, Matthew. "Cultivating 'Sensibility' in Writing Program Administration." WPA: Program Administration, vol. 35, no. 2, 2012, pp. 38–54.

hooks, bell. Teaching to Transgress. Routledge, 1994.

Horner, Bruce. Terms of Work for Composition: A Materialist Critique. SUNY, 2000.

Kerkham, Lyn. "Embodied Literacies and a Poetics of Place." English Teaching: Practice and Critique, vol. 10, no. 3, 2011, pp. 9–25.

Kirsch, Gesa E., Faye S. Maor, Lance Massey, Lee Nickoson-Massey, and Mary P. Sheridan Rabideau, editors. *Feminism and Composition: A Critical Sourcebook.* Bedford/St. Martin's, 2003.

Kopelson, Karen. "Dis/Integrating the Gay/Queer Binary: 'Reconstructed Identity Politics' for a Performative Pedagogy." *College English*, vol. 65, no. 1, 2002, pp. 17–35.

Kuppers, Petra. "Moving Bodies." *The Teacher's Body: Embodiment, Authority, and Identity in the Academy*, edited by Diane P. Freeman and Martha Stoddard Holmes. SUNY Press, 2003.

Lave, Jean, and Etienne Wenger. *Situated Learning: Legitimate Peripheral Participation.* Cambridge University Press, 1997.

Ong, Walter. "The Writer's Audience is Always a Fiction." *PMLA*, vol. 90, no. 1, 1975, pp. 9–21.

Phelan, Peggy. "Dance and the History of Hysteria." *Corporealities: Dancing Knowledge, Culture, and Power*, edited by Susan L. Foster. Routledge, 1996.

Ross, Janice. "The Instructable Body: Student Bodies from Classrooms to Prisons." *Knowing Bodies, Moving Minds: Towards Embodied Teaching and Learning*, edited by Loira Bresler, Kluwer, 2004.

Shor, Ira. *When Students Have Power.* University of Chicago Press, 1996.

Sini, Carlos. *The Ethics of Writing.* SUNY Press, 2009.

Thoreau, Henry David. "Walking." *Project Gutenberg,* updated November 3, 2010.

Chapter 11. "Who Decides My Grade?" Reflections on Team Teaching and Peer Mentoring in First-Year Composition

Christopher Garland

University of Southern Mississippi

This essay reflects on my experiences as a mentee and mentor instructor in a team-teaching writing program. Although a number of essays and research articles have been written about mentoring teachers at the college level, comparatively little has been written about team teaching in composition classes. The co-taught classroom enables different approaches to teaching first-year composition, challenges students to adjust to a collective pedagogy, and fosters a dynamic that teaches lessons applicable both in and out of the classroom. Along with cultivating a closer relationship with their individual *graders*, a co-taught class compels the students to develop relationships with the other instructors. Drawing on time in the University of Florida's University Writing Program—where I had the opportunity to be involved in multiple co-taught writing classes—and assorted interactions with students, fellow graduate instructors, and faculty involved with the design and implementation of co-taught courses during that time, this reflective essay seeks to consider the pedagogical successes, drawbacks, and unique opportunities that come out of the team teaching environment. In this first part of the essay, I will address some of the research (across a number of disciplines) that has gone into the efficacy of team teaching. In the second part of the essay, I will talk in more detail about my own experience as a co-teacher and mentor.

First, however, I thought it important to talk about how critical co-teaching has been to me as a writing teacher. During the eight years I have spent designing and teaching classes at the University of Florida and the University of Southern Mississippi, my approach to teaching has shifted from merely imparting the *right* knowledge to actively working with students in a collaborative environment that incorporates reading, writing, and critical thinking. This shift has been the most profound in my growth as a teacher, and it is directly related to what I learnt from being in the classroom with other teachers—some of whom had more experience teaching writing than I did, some of whom had less. The co-taught classroom requires adaptability as well as the ability to collaborate on syllabi, assignment sheets, rubrics, and the various other documents that help us shape our writing courses; in this environment, it's crucial to be able to compromise on pedagogical approaches and thinking about shifting classroom dynamics. In practical terms, due to the influence of co-teachers, I have gone from spending a significant amount of the class period lecturing about concepts and providing specific feedback for students to creating a classroom environment where students both analyze and create various texts. This does not mean that I have done away with the important work of leading discussion, introducing ideas that challenge the students, and giving suggestions and revisions regarding their work. Rather, I have come to see the class period as a time when students can do something that underpins the learning process, whether analyzing an online advertisement that requires a short oral presentation, assessing the logic of a feasibility report, or introducing a counterargument to a section of a proposal. It is not enough for a teacher to be passionate and invested in teaching; the students also must have a significant stake in shaping their own learning environment. With this objective in mind—especially when this objective is shared with co-teachers—a more collaborative learning space can be created.

Another part of my growth as a professor (and as a benefit of co-teaching) has been the importance of providing context—historical, political, and cultural—for the issues we are addressing in the classroom. Again, this was something that I was able to develop further when teaching writing with others. Teaching alongside people who bring their own specific interests to the practical and theoretical aspects of writing studies—say, for example, a research agenda on the writing of prison inmates or the rhetoric of the Mississippi Delta blues—further pushes on the notion of context. With the benefit of multiple instructors who have their own distinct knowledge bases, students can then build on that knowledge to critically engage with different texts, genres, and technical documents. In class conversations, we can then model the process of learning on not only *analysis* of the text but also on how writings and images are produced, circulated, and received by their respective audiences. (And the best of those discussions allow the students to make dynamic connections between their own writing, the texts that we are analyzing, and the one-on-one conversations they have had with each of the co-teachers.) We recently experienced success with this pedagogical approach in a class on the visual culture of death and dying. From images of the September 11, 2001, attacks to cross-cultural *memento mori* (for example, comparing the use of human skulls in contemporary Vodou in Haiti and the U.S. with the skull as motif in 17th-century Dutch painting), we considered the relationship between cultural, religious, and national contexts and the universal experience of death and dying. More generally, in working with a broad range of student writers, we emphasized the necessity of considering the audience and the information being communicated not only in their work but also when considering the construction of other forms of writing. Drawing on the particular knowledge I am committed to asking students to consider the networks to which texts belong and what this can reveal about the relationship between individuals, communities, and entire nations.

My own identity as a foreigner also informs my teaching philosophy and my experience as a co-teacher. I would argue that an instructor's foreign identity offers a valuable and compelling avenue for teaching and learning in the U.S. university classroom. The foreign instructor is a conduit to a world outside the

American educational experience, synthesizing his or her own background in classrooms abroad with a distinctive set of pedagogical approaches shaped by the U.S. tertiary system. Because I did not attend high school in the U.S., my students' prior experiences with writing and communication in an educational setting are often alien to me. But rather than being an uncomfortable impediment or even an insurmountable obstacle, this *disconnect* has enabled various productive teaching moments. Moreover, I was initially helped in this process by learning from my co-teachers about their experiences as high school students and undergraduates at colleges in the U.S. As my first experience with first-year composition was in a co-taught class, I was at first reluctant to *stand out* to the students. My accent was noticeable in comparison to my fellow American co-teachers: this made me self-conscious that I would be seen as someone with less understanding about the American college classroom. But I received encouragement from my co-teachers about *embracing* the difference. I was the first foreign teacher that many of the students had ever had, and I couldn't help but wonder how this affected my ethos when leading the classroom discussion. But by employing both micro-level (showing the use of different terminology from other *Englishes* to demonstrate context, for example) and macro-level (introducing a foreigner's viewpoint of the U.S. and this country's effect on the rest of the world) distinctions, the complexity of fronting the American classroom as an outsider facilitates many positive opportunities. Moreover, being foreign offers an opportunity to connect with the increasingly diverse students who make up U.S. college classrooms. However, I'm not sure I would've come to embrace my foreign identity in the classroom so quickly without the encouragement of my American co-teachers.

My first experience with co-teaching came in an unexpected manner. On starting graduate school, I was given two teaching assignments, one of which was for a first-year writing classroom. The director of the writing program put me in contact with a mentor for that class, and it wasn't until that point that I realized that I would be teaching with someone else. At the end of that first semester, I realized how lucky I was to be put in that situation. I wouldn't have developed confidence in leading classroom discussion and shaping in-class writing assignments. Moreover, it wasn't just the experience of learning from the mentor: I was teaching alongside two other new graduate students, both of whom had more teaching experience than I had. However, there is research on the efficacy of the co-taught classroom. "Teaching with a Peer: A Comparison of Two Models of Student Teaching" compares two models of student teaching: where one student teacher works with a mentor teacher and where two student teachers work with one mentor. The latter is closer to what I will be discussing in the second half of the essay, and the study concluded that while there were some drawbacks in the three-teacher model, overall there is the opportunity for dialogue between the co-teachers, more support due to the fact that the student teachers can draw on the mentor's toolkit, and collaboration that comes from beyond a one-on-one dynamic. "Co-teaching: An Overview of the Past, a Glimpse at the Present, and Considerations for the Future," Marilyn Friend, Monica Reising, and Lynne Cook, framed by their experiences in special education, define co-teaching as "an instructional delivery approach in which a classroom teacher and a special education teacher (or other special services professional) share responsibility for planning, delivering, and evaluating instruction for a group of students" (6). While writing out of the context of the special education classroom, Friend, Reising, and Cook also succinctly describe the objectives of the co-teaching classroom: in co-teaching, "the teachers strive to create a classroom community in which all students are valued members, and they develop innovative teaching strategies that would not be possible if only teacher was present" (6).

Building on parts of Friend, Reising, and Cook's seminal study, Nancy Bacharach and Teresa Heck's "Co-Teaching in Higher Education" focused on 16 university level co-taught classes and took into account the preparation of faculty for co-teaching. The study showed that the "co-teaching experience provided an energizing opportunity for faculty to renew their passion for their profession" (25). Moreover, faculty, after being part of a co-taught class, unanimously assert that they "had an enriching experience in which they learned new material and instructional strategies . . . [while becoming more] reflective about their teaching since decisions about how and what to teach had to be negotiated rather than prescribed by one individual" (25). Looking at another discipline, music education, Stephen J. Paul addressed how co-teaching relates to the motivation of an individual to become a teacher is related to a collective identity: "In simple terms, to become a teacher, a person must first want to become a member of the group 'teachers.' He or she must learn to do 'teacherly' things—planning and presenting lessons, evaluating students progress, diagnosing student problems and prescribing solutions . . . " (73). Where I learnt to do "teacherly things" came through the co-taught classroom, and it shaped how I would mentor fellow teachers in the future.

From my experience, here's how the co-teaching classroom plays out: After introducing myself, mentioning some of the primary goals of this first-year composition class, and assuring the students that my intent is to reward improvement over the course of the semester, I have one last task: To explain to the 19 students seated in front of me why there is not one but four instructors here today. Turning to my right, I ask my co-teachers to introduce themselves: Shoniqua, an M.A. student in Gender Studies who has just moved South after graduating from Penn State; Emily, another M.A. student from Miami, who is focused on Children's Literature and is just three years older than some of the students in this room; Vincent, a journalist turned creative writer from California who has moved to Florida to complete an MFA. I then tell the students that each of the instructors will be responsible for a particular *module* or *unit*, selling the fact that having four instructors in the classroom will give this class the kind of student/teacher ratio that is extremely rare at a public institution. Most of all I emphasize how as co-instructors we work together as a cohesive team teaching group.

I take comfort in the idea that the initially perplexed looks on their faces are a reflection of not only this news but also of shellshock from the first couple of days at one of the country's largest universities. I reiterate that this is an opportunity for students to work closely with an instructor to improve their writing skills— not only for their college careers but also for other future endeavors: graduate school, the workplace. I don't tell them that none of my co-teachers have taught before. I don't tell them that this system is as imperfect as any other pedagogical approach. I do tell them that there are more of us (instructors) than they'll ever have in any other class, and I have seen it work very well, even brilliantly at times. I don't tell them that we might not always agree on teaching practices, but I do tell them that I have taught in a number of different environments, and this one I love the most. I then ask them if they have any questions, and I wait for one that inevitably arrives every semester: "Who decides my grade?"

Like all teaching, team teaching begins before we stand in front of our students on that first day of the semester. However, the *prep time* process is one of the primary differences between a single-instructor and the co-taught course. Whether or not incoming graduate teaching assistants (the mentees) to UF's University Writing Program have teaching experience, they are viewed as a vital proponent of the shape of the course: primarily in contributing to the syllabus. In this way, mentees take ownership of the course at this key moment in the course's development. Moreover, particularly for graduate students with limited or no prior teaching experience, working with a mentor who has taught numerous first-year composition classes helps to alleviate that very specific source of anxiety: the prospect of standing in front of a class filled with college students for the first time.

My co-teacher Emily's anxiety about this prospect was particularly acute because she had been an undergraduate at the same institution less than a year before. One of her main worries was whether the students would "take her seriously" due to her age. From our first meetings during those weeks leading up to the semester, Emily's nervousness about leading a class discussion was palpable. Although she would not be leading discussion of the first readings, she was concerned about her ability to do so later in the semester. And while it is not a magic bullet for alleviating a first-time teacher's stress, the team teaching environment provides ongoing support throughout the semester, and this atmosphere is integral at the outset. As many of my new co-teachers have attested, the prospect of that first day standing in front of a room of freshmen is scarier than the reality: After the first productive peer-review session or in-class writing session, the new co-teacher is visibly more confident. In the co-taught classroom, the teacher is not left alone to figure it all out. There is an instructor who has taught the course numerous times before and co-teachers who are, to use a cliché, in the same boat. Together, we ruminate on age-old questions about teaching writing: how does one encourage revision? How do we connect the readings to the concepts that we are attempting to teach? But, unlike the vast majority of first-writing classes, these questions are contemplated amongst teachers in a group setting, and the conversation continues throughout the semester. As a group, we return time and again to this meta-analysis of the course.

Prior to our first class session, Emily asked questions about how I had taught the class before, but she also looked to her co-teachers and fellow new graduate students for advice. One particularly fruitful conversation concerned destabilizing the teacher (authority figure)/freshman student (passive receptacle) relationship. Reflecting on their experiences as writers in both high school and college, Shoniqua, Vincent, and Emily talked about the type of writing class they would ideally create. All three expressed a desire to draw on some pedagogical approaches from high school and college; however, unlike when this discussion occurs among new instructors who are teaching a class *solo*, these teachers would be implementing a pedagogical synthesis of sorts. For her part, Emily stated that she wasn't invested in presenting herself as an *expert*, but rather as someone who possessed valuable experience as a writer, as someone who could facilitate the growth of students' writing confidence.

One of the most visible ways that the co-taught class impacts the student is via feedback on their work from more than one instructor. For example, when we held in-class peer-review sessions, I encouraged the co-teachers to seek out students who weren't in the instructor's grading group. The first time we did this, my initial thought was that students would complain about getting "mixed messages" about, say, the scope of their argument. One instructor might suggest a narrower focus, while another might encourage a widening of the essay's critical lens. Inevitably, differences in opinions about the direction of a student's essay arose, but this was rarely detrimental to the student. In fact, it encouraged the kind of dialectical thinking that enables a more thoughtful, dynamic, and nuanced argument to emerge on paper. The student must both respond to and consider incorporating information from more than one (non-peer) reviewer. In many cases, I saw students integrating this feedback through a variety of nuanced and often surprising methods. "Vincent suggested that I include a counterargument earlier in my essay," one student said to me, "and Emily said it would work better towards the end. (Their feedback) made me realize how important this particular argument is. . . . I am going to make the essay respond more directly to (this person's) article, and break it down point-by-point." The combination of one-on-one/small group interaction and the different instructors' critical perspectives provide a particularly fruitful writing environment for the first-year composition student.

Of course, there is the constant concern about grading papers—more precisely, how students perceive the grading process in the co-taught composition course. Students who are resistant to the co-taught class are often preoccupied with the subjectivity and power involved in grading. Rather than trying to persuade students that the grading would be as *fair* as in any other single-instructor classroom environment, at the beginning of the semester we describe the process behind grading in the co-taught class. This description is not as simple as telling the students that we discuss the work of each student and have an ongoing conversation about the aims of the course; it is also a process of presenting to the student-writers the practical implementations of the co-taught classroom.

During the first week, we divide the class into grading groups and assign each instructor a group. We have created these groups through two different ways: some semesters we randomly divide the class into three or four groups, depending on the number of co-teachers. In other semesters, we assign a diagnostic writing assignment—usually a personal narrative focused on the student's previous experiences with writing—and then divide the class after reading through these assignments. The purpose here (and this is something we reiterate to students) is not to identify those so-called *strong* and *weak* writers on the basis of some traditional form and content criteria but rather to give the other instructors a group of student-writers from dissimilar writing backgrounds. Student groups may range from those students who are paralyzed by word counts; students who believe writing *skill* is some inherent gift; those who are determined to write *just enough* to get through the class.

Particularly for those graduate instructors teaching freshman composition for the first time, this exposure to students with varying levels of confidence in their own ability as writers is a foundational experience. Meeting with the students in the smaller grading groups and discussing with them their own writing histories invariably begins a later conversation—usually and enthusiastically after the class period—among the co-teachers about pedagogy. Often this conversation focused on the necessity of not seeing first-year writing students as some monolithic group. Especially in the case of new graduate instructors, the use of conferencing to directly address the needs of each student writer helps emphasize the diversity of our student-writers, and allows the co-teacher to see what motivates the student writer. The smaller grading groups also allow the co-teacher to foster the notion of being part of a writing community: like our first-year students, we teachers also agonize over our own writing. Even without prompting the new co-teachers in this direction, in the co-taught classes I regularly see an instructor's reference to her own writing history as an extremely effective pedagogical tool. Vincent, for example, captured the students' attention talking about form and his own transition from full-time journalist to a poet in an MFA program (and the intimidating environment of the graduate school workshop!). By sharing with our students our own experiences with editors and peer feedback we demonstrate empathy about the constant challenge of writing. This *thing* is not easy, and we are struggling with the process of crafting sentences, paragraphs, and essays (not to mention the related research), too.

Once the co-teachers know the students they are responsible for grading the real strengths of the co-taught writing class become readily apparent to both student and instructor. First, the student is going to have more opportunities to interact with the person "who decides the grade," and the instructor has a greater number of times to use the one-on-one setting for particular pedagogical ends. Also, in emphasizing to students that while each instructor is responsible for a particular assignment, the structure, content, and objectives of the class were developed in a team environment. This coordinated construction of the reading list, syllabus, and assignments gives each instructor a sense of ownership of the course as a whole. For example, even if Shoniqua wasn't the lead instructor on the rhetorical analysis, through her interactions with students during in-class activities related to the assignment, she has been an integral part of the teaching of the module.

In weekly meetings with Emily, Shoniqua, and Vincent, we discuss the development of the student-writers. Rather than solely focusing on the students' grades, we begin by talking about the class holistically: how different students have reacted to particular in-class assignments, what we might change (for example, how we could arrange a peer-review session and utilize all four teachers at once), and adjustments we could make to the readings in order to emphasize pertinent concepts. (Emily, in particular, helped her co-teachers select useful readings that drew together many of the course's core concepts.) This collaboration often leads into talk about the success of the most recent assignment, and, by extension, what grades have been given. Because during in-class activities we circulate—consciously attending to students who are not in our respective grading groups—our collective concern is not limited to just the individual grading group. For instance, because Vincent spent some time talking to Sean, a student in my grading group, about incorporating counter-arguments to his paper, Vincent asks me about Sean's essay. Or Emily, who led the module, asks about one of Shoniqua's students, Robert, who had missed the peer review session. Even though the final grade of each student is the responsibility of the individual grader, the progression of the student-writers comes about through a collective interaction amongst the co-teachers.

Team teaching is not a perfect science. Instructors are not always going to agree about the form and content of classes, and not every instructor is ready to engage in the type of compromise that is inherent in the co-teaching environment. However, the majority of discord and disagreement has had unexpectedly productive outcomes. I have seen a reluctant co-teacher come to see the value of drawing from another instructor's experience even if the instructors disagree about a variety of issues, and I have benefitted from new instructors challenging my default approaches to grading and teaching. Through the team teaching model, I have been lucky enough to witness anxious teachers fall in love with the first-year writing classroom, and this enthusiasm, in turn, has had a direct, positive effect on our student-writers.

Works Cited

Bacharach, Nancy, Teresa Washut Heck, and Kathryn Dahlbert. "Co-Teaching in Higher Education." *Journal of College Teaching & Learning*, vol. 5, no. 3, 2008, pp. 9–16.

Paul, Stephen J. "The Effects of Peer Teaching Experiences on the Professional Teacher Role of Undergraduate Instrumental Music Education Majors." *Bulletin of the Council for Research in Music Education*, no. 137, 1998, pp. 73–92.

Section 3: What We Write

Chapter 12. Introduction

Lillian E. Craton

Lander University

Every fall semester, my English 101 students undertake a series of formal debates as a way to practice their rhetorical skills. Topics are drawn from student life. For instance, should our dry campus become wet? Does our university need a football team? One group of students in each class debates whether the university should maintain its current general education distribution requirements. Though the topic initially seems dry, it often leads to one of our most impassioned discussions.

Designed to foster reflection on the purpose behind students' coursework during freshman year, this topic has the added benefit of drawing in other voices to reinforce my sales pitch for the value of our course. Moreover, it gives me a window into students' assumptions about my class. These assumptions can be troubling, and the students charged with interrogating our general education system often question the value of higher education itself. They imagine dark motives for institutional decisions. General education coursework, they say, is just a way for universities to lengthen the degree program and make more money from their students.

These conspiracy theories seem silly to educators tuned in to pedagogy and accreditation requirements. Nonetheless, they highlight the importance of communicating with students about the reasons we do what we do in the classroom. Though writing is not something one simply memorizes—it requires practice and coaching, as does any skill—students perceive and resent the repetition of high school material in university coursework. They bemoan a lack of purpose behind many of their general education courses. Beyond checking off boxes required for graduation, many students don't understand what they are supposed to be getting out of the freshman experience.

If I want students to invest in my class and assignments, I must be able to articulate the value of this work in a way they find meaningful, to communicate the learning outcomes driving our activity. Fortunately, the English 101 debaters assigned to defend our gen-ed program help me do so. Last semester, the pro-gen-ed team won their debate with a simple argument: Did their classmates actually feel *ready* yet? At the start of freshman year, did they feel like they had the skills necessary to succeed in difficult classes in their major, on the job market, in careers? No? That's okay, my students argued, because the purpose of general education coursework is to prepare us to succeed.

I agree, and so do the authors in this section. The essays provide borrow-worthy activities, themes, or assignments that you might consider adopting in your own classroom. More importantly, though, they provide a model for deep thinking and intentionality within a course design driven by concern for students' long-term academic and professional success. Such modeling is useful, not only for our teaching, but also for students' learning. Writing about writing for the *International Journal for the Scholarship of Teaching and Learning*, Miriam Carey argues that purposeful teaching can create intentional, integrative learners primed to succeed:

> Intentional learning implies a greater degree of student self-awareness regarding the importance (or not) of what is being learned and the best methods of learning for the particular individual. . . . Integrative learning implies the ability to apply learning outside the classroom in the broader arenas of other course work and life in general; to make connections between the academic theories or processes learned in one course to other courses and hopefully to their larger life in the *real world*.

Carey suggests that integrative learning may "facilitate better academic performance" and "foster life-long learning." Furthermore, most students "can be encouraged to develop both of these predispositions and thus find, in their learning experience, greater success and satisfaction as they would define it themselves." To become intentional and integrative learners, students need help finding connections between the work in front of them and the long-term success they hope to achieve.

These five essays trace those connections. The section begins with an exploration of how our approach to source material may help students grasp the purpose and value of research. Lynée Lewis Gaillet considers the value of primary sources: archival research not only in academic libraries but also the less formal information centers offered by families and communities. Undergraduates often prejudge research as tedious or pointless. However, true research requires more than a Google search; in an era of instant access to facts, writing teachers must remind students of the differences between information and knowledge. By delving into hometown archives, Gaillet's students learn the process of research while also reflecting on the act of creating knowledge—and having a lot of fun.

Just as hometown archives give new purpose to the act of research, an active digital life reminds students of the real purpose of writing: to inform or affect an audience. Kathryn Crowther taps into her students' enthusiasm for digital communication by assigning blogs as part of their composition coursework. The assignment reinforces skills like self-presentation and audience-analysis while building a sense of community among first-year students. Because bloggers have creative control over the presentation of their ideas but receive feedback through comment tools, blogs encourage students to take ownership of their own writing and accept critique. Ultimately, the combination of wisdom and personal connections built online reshapes the classroom dynamic.

Even engaged students may struggle to rise to the daily challenges of a full college courseload. Lisa Whalen details an assignment that accomplishes central goals of writing coursework—understanding the stages of the writing process, conducting and incorporating research, fine-tuning language and structure—while also teaching students how to be students beyond English 101. Whalen's students use collaborative learning and reflection to explore topics related to academic success. The approach has value for students at all levels but has been particularly meaningful for underprepared students.

A clear sense of the professional payoff of education provides the motivation to struggle through academic challenges. Abigail Scheg asks her students to research the professional audiences and rhetorical situations they are likely to encounter after graduation. Students spend most of their writing-lives responding to the demands of their chosen careers; as nurses, teachers, or FBI agents, they must adapt to differing goals and expectations that govern communication within their fields. Writing projects tied to career goals help students see and access the practical value of composition coursework.

Finally, Matthew Paproth explores a popular theme in composition courses: food. As an essential part of life and a reflection of family traditions, food is a relatable topic that taps into personal experiences. It also, however, opens up cultural, social, scientific, and ethical questions for student research. By connecting personal taste to larger issues—deconstructing their Thanksgiving feasts, for instance, or considering why they perceive some animals as more palatable than others—students practice analytical skills in a comforting but challenging context.

Work Cited

Carey, Miriam. "In the Valley of the Giants: Cultivating Intentionality and Integration." *International Journal for the Scholarship of Teaching and Learning*, vol. 6, no. 1, 2012, p. 7.

Chapter 13. Primary Research in the Vertical Writing Curriculum

Lynée Lewis Gaillet

Georgia State University

"Weekly, daily, hourly, anything called news was already archival."
—*Goodman, The Cookbook Collector 249*

Archival research, always a staple of academic inquiry, has recently received much broader attention. From Henry Louis Gates' PBS series focused on African American genealogy to Ken Burns' body of archival documentaries to the sheer number of historical novels listed on Goodreads.com, it's clear that archival research can be commercially successful and downright entertaining. Primary investigation often involves following a fun trail of clues, whether the origin of the project is a family artifact, community story, or a serendipitous find. Unfortunately, however, academicians often manage to stifle this most interesting aspect of our research in publications and rarely explain the process we find so engaging to either readers or students. How might we share at least a little bit of this excitement, storytelling, and passion with both our academic readers and our students? More importantly, how do we teach primary research skills and associated writing forms to our students so that they might become passionate about their own writing and in the process find their academic voices, learn to write for specific audiences, and develop research and writing practices that are transferable?

For years, I've shared my academic passion for archival research methodologies and methods with PhD students, those researching dissertations, but recently I have come to the realization that primary research answers a multitude of needs in undergraduate and masters-level writing instruction as well. When students select primary research topics that hold a personal interest, they quickly take ownership of the project, seek archival evidence to support their claims, and write for a targeted audience. The kind of pedagogy I am advocating avoids pitfalls of plagiarism and boredom in the writing class. It teaches writing and research skills that that are adaptable across the curriculum, and prepares students for both academic and workplace writing. In this chapter, I will first discuss extending the vertical writing curriculum in writing pedagogy, then describe a writing class based on primary research, provide some assignments, and offer individual students' work as illustration. I have taught a version of this class in courses earmarked expository writing and advanced composition, but this approach works well in beginning composition courses, too. I recently co-authored (with Michelle Eble) a first-year writing text grounded in primary investigation, *Primary Research and*

Writing: People, Places, and Spaces (Routledge 2016), a primer designed to introduce beginning writing students across the disciplines to the value of archival
research. I find it paradoxical that students fully understand the concepts and
praxis of secondary research without having any real knowledge of primary
investigation. Given the recent scholarly attention focused not only on theories
but also methods of archival research (Glenn and Enoch; Donahue and Moon;
Kirsch and Rohan; Hayden; Buehl, Chute, and Fields), pedagogical implications
of primary investigation in lower division courses now seem ripe for exploration.

The Vertical Writing Curriculum

Extending the vertical curriculum—that's a common phrase in composition
scholarship and the goal of writing programs across the country. Teachers and
Writing Program Administrators (WPA) regularly argue for the development
and reexamination of courses in the advanced writing program—a curriculum
area that is often hard to define, evidenced ironically in both the range and scarcity of texts available for adoption in advanced writing courses, both undergraduate and graduate. The difficulty in defining and shaping composition instruction
between the bookends of first-year writing courses and graduate courses in
composition theory/pedagogy designed for TAs who teach first-year writing
is often problematic at best, as examined in works such as Linda K. Shamoon,
Rebecca Moore Howard, Sandra Jamieson, and Robert A. Schwegler's excellent
and groundbreaking collection *Coming of Age: The Advanced Writing Curriculum*
(2000). However, seventeen years later, teachers, departments, and book publishers alike still have trouble defining how to teach advanced writing courses.
In part, this ambiguity is what makes these courses attractive to teachers. We can
take an existing class and give it our own imprint—as suggested in the various
course plans presented in the *Coming of Age* collection. Contributors to the present volume, *Writing Pathways to Student Success*, certainly present pedagogical
ideas that are applicable across the undergraduate curriculum. In her chapter, for
instance, Sarah O'Connor suggests that we address common problems in writing
courses by helping students understand

- The role of civil discourse in a community
- The importance of identifying the main point in an argument
- The value of knowing the full context of an issue
- The value of listening to and respecting multiple points of views
- The importance of questioning what we hear and read, along with an idea
  of the questions to ask.

These are important and universal considerations as we design a variety of different composition pedagogies and expand the curriculum to include contemporary
theories of writing and research. Keeping O'Connor's points in mind also helps us
decide how to refocus existing and new themes in composition classes.

For example, I regularly teach my department's expository writing course, a class that has been on the books for decades but one that teachers always ponder how to teach. Publishing reps have given up trying to sell us a text for this course. However, I love the class for its ambiguity. Yes, the course has published goals (addressing style, form, structure, etc.) but *how* to teach to those "aims" is left open to interpretation. In the past, I've taught the course focused on the history of the essay, as a class in academic publishing, even as a kind of special topics in journalism and exposition. But the last time I taught expository writing, I organized the course with a focus on archival research methods and primary investigation, an approach that is attractive to students from across the disciplines and that prepares students for success in both academic and workplace writing. Here is the class description from my syllabus:

> Historians of rhetorical practices, along with other scholars and those interested in the past, examine archives in an effort to seek nuanced, complicated tales—ones moored to their own times and cultural exigencies. Our adoption of recovery and revision methodologies often leads us to reexamine traditional "truths"; this important work depends on a plurality of research methods and the willingness of the researcher to carefully (re)consider venues and genres for disseminating our work. In this course, we will learn to become "archivists with an attitude"—scholars who base contemporary scholarship on primary investigations, and more importantly scholars who have something original, interesting, and pointed to add to academic conversations.

In this class design, students learn how to select topics that have personal appeal for the researcher/writer, follow a list of steps and suggestions to find archives (both physical and digital), visit collections, and explore ways to analyze findings and introduce the results into existing scholarly conversations. The researcher examines his or her reasons for conducting research and personal beliefs and biases throughout this process. Students may be initially unsure exactly where we're headed, but most embrace the opportunity to blaze meaningful trails, and the resulting writing is engaging, unique, interesting, and perhaps most importantly inspired. Even when it falls a bit short of the students' initial goals, the work is so much better than the majority of student writing I've read since I began teaching over thirty years ago. While many students write about family and community issues, the class offers opportunities for investigating workplace issues as well.

One of my students was rather uninterested in the class until we began discussing how primary research is essential on the job. He works as a deliverer at a national pizza chain. Throughout the course he expressed great displeasure at how the computer in another state dictates how many delivery persons an outlet needs to staff during a specific shift, regardless of the weather conditions. Together, we came up with a research project based on his dissatisfaction—in an attempt to change work practices. He studied the computer data over a given time period and successfully made a recommendation to headquarters about adjusting staffing in downtown Atlanta markets on rainy Sunday nights. He scored big points at work with this project. Another student who was unhappy with management practices at the restaurant where she worked offered her services to help the establishment write a policy and procedure manual for wait staff—informed in part by experience, observation, and interviews with other employees. These projects, along with the familial and community projects described below, demonstrate value of archival investigation across the disciplines.

While I have adapted existing classes to include archival research and occasionally taught both graduate and undergraduate special topics courses in archival research methods, my ultimate goal was to have a regular course addressing this methodology in the course catalog. Fall 2016, I taught the first "on the books" section of ENGL4521/6521: Archival Research Methods. The projects emerging in this class followed the same patterns found in the 3000 level class. Topics ran the gamut, reflecting students' interests and access in family records, work-place practices, and community issues. What I quickly learned is that archival investigation is inviting and fascinating for ALL researchers, regardless of their level of training or experience because they are vested from the first moment in their projects, and in many instances finally have an opportunity to research topics that they may have been thinking about for quite a while. Consider this project description from a semester-long student project titled "American Song":

> "You Are My Sunshine" is a part of the American songbook, alongside favorites like Mildred J. Hill's ditty "Happy Birthday," and Woody Guthrie's protest song "This Land is Your Land." It is also part of my family history, for my family contends that my great grandfather wrote this song, a claim of some heated dispute. This dispute is what led to my interest in pursuing research on the song and its subsequent avenues. I feel compelled, however, to state up front that while I have a dog in the fight and I believe in that dog, I am aware that others could say the same. Moreover, I must note that the songs status as a source of contention that so accurately speaks to the topics surrounding privilege and opportunity (socio-economic) common during the early twentieth century, really fuels my interest in solving this riddle. (Jessica Rose)

Jessica uses the opportunity for archival research as an invitation to solve an historical family "riddle," and in the process writes a wonderful, personal case study illustrating universal and contemporary copyright law, author attribution, and royalty issues. She uses as her primary evidence, interviews and artifacts, historical records and legal documents.

Another student, Mandy Ryan expanded a very personal familial project into a case study significant to historical investigations of mental illness. As Mandy explains,

> For the [archival research] course, students chose one research project for the semester that involved using physical and digital archives. I choose a series of letters written by my great-grandmother who had been briefly institutionalized by her husband in the late 1940s. I spent months researching her history in various archives trying to trace her career path and subsequent admittance. I realized that her story was a small part of a much larger picture of women who had been silenced through ECT, so I turned my focus to other letters and admittance procedures, and I researched early psychiatric practices. I am beyond proud of my final project and even more excited that it isn't finished, but the beginning of a much larger research project that I intend to continue working on and growing with.

Similarly, moving from a familial project to a community one with much wider appeal, Emily Kimbell describes her project investigating a local/historical college in her hometown. This project will resonate with researchers interested in feminist studies and the history of educational practices, as well as those readers wanting to know more about Newnan, GA:

> My research project focuses on College Temple, a late 19th century women's college located in my hometown of Newnan, Georgia. College Temple first opened in 1853 and was purportedly the first college to grant women a master's degree. Throughout its thirty-six year existence, College Temple developed a preparatory department, served as a Civil War hospital, and transitioned into a co-educational facility. My journey to learn more about the school has brought me to both physical and digital archives housed at universities, historical societies, and local libraries. Throughout my research, I've developed a connection with the women who attended College Temple and discovered their writings, their lives, and their impact. My class project has turned into a life-long research endeavor—one that leads me back home to reflect on my community, my historical influences, and in turn, myself.

These example illustrates two recurring themes that I've discovered in teaching archival research methods: (1) students ALWAYS take on projects that I could never have anticipated or assigned and (2) the work is rarely finished at the end of the term. Most projects end with subsections titled some version of "Where I Will Go Next." Students leave the course with plans for continuing their investigations and plans for disseminating their findings more broadly. For me, this is the most exciting facet of this pedagogy.

Be the Archivists

In the advanced undergraduate writing class and the split-level 4000/6000 level course, I adopt the 2010 collection *Working in the Archives*, co-edited by Ramsey, Sharer, L'Eplattenier, and Mastrangelo, as the class text. Contributors to this volume tackle the practical issues associated with seeking primary documents, discuss the role serendipity plays in archival searches, and explore the way academic investigation shifts when the search is online. Specific "how to" chapters offer concrete suggestions for investigating photographs, letters, and student writing. And other contributors provide taxonomies for organizing research findings, personal accounts about archival research methods and findings, and ways advice for becoming an archivist-researcher. Collectively, the authors introduce researchers to archivists' terms and practices. I've been researching archives for 30 years but didn't understand until reading this volume the real meaning behind primary research terms such as "original order," "finding aids," "provenance," or "preservation principles." *Working in the Archives* changed my perception of not only the role that the archivist plays in the researcher's work, but also how I might recast my teaching and scholarship in ways that lead me to teach students how to be archivists, not just researchers. I have a great upcoming project to test out my new knowledge.

I've had two boxes of my long-retired (and now deceased) dissertation director's papers sitting in my office for years. I have not opened those boxes—although I wanted to. These materials and manuscripts are related to Dr. Winifred Horner's important book, *Scottish Rhetoric: The American Connection*. I didn't open them because I was afraid that I didn't have the necessary skills to catalog the materials. They've been staring at me for a long time, and for the first time I felt equipped after reading *Working in the Archives* to open the box without disturbing the original order, to create a finding aid, store the items appropriately in acid free folders, reproduce and then purge the collection of toxic materials like newspaper clippings. In short, I am now ready to be the archivists *and* the researcher—and I have enlisted one of the undergraduate students in my class to work with me so she can learn basic archival principles to use in her own forthcoming projects. Learning with my students is what keeps teaching alive for me, and in classes based on primary research, I learn just as much with and from my students as they do. In addition to learning how to gather and interpret primary research, my students have learned how to archive materials, including: family artifacts (photos, newspaper clippings, public records, and letters), materials of monetary value (loose stamps that were catalogued and appraised), historical items (civil war ammunition, pamphlets, and flyers), and municipal documents (government papers, maps, and committee meeting minutes). Impressive accomplishments indeed.

I will remember these students (and many others like them) along with their work long after the courses are over, but more importantly, I think they will remember what they have learned in these writing course as well, apply archival research methodologies and primary investigation skills to other academic ventures, and use what they have learned in real-world and workplace writing situations.

First-Year Writing

To truly discuss a vertical curriculum, we have to include first-year writing—and even high school instruction—in examinations of archival research. We need to think about ways we teach writing and research to students who aren't remotely interested (and perhaps shouldn't be) in traditional research methods and patchwork writing. As mentioned above, *Primary Research and Writing: People, Places, and Spaces* is designed to introduce first-year writers to original research. Although researching and writing about primary sources only enriches course goals for first-year writing instruction, like the ones advocated by the Council of Writing Program Administrators, I realize that the tasks we are asking both students and teachers to do are alien, a bit scary, and sometimes initially uncomfortable—simply because these assignments are unconventional in the beginning writing class. However, where these tasks *are* everyday and common is in the workplace (as my student mentioned above found out delivering pizzas), and in other academic classes. Subjecting students at every level to a variety of research methods, asking them not only to study the basic principles and how-tos of primary research methods but also engage in original research projects is exciting, albeit hard, work—the kinds of activities ultimately required across the curriculum and in our students' careers, whether they pursue academic positions or not. Most professionals don't write traditional research reports based on one kind of research methodology except to provide background, couch findings and analysis. The ways we traditionally introduce inquiry in writing classes and the kinds of projects we require are, in the worst case, *just* academic. They have no life, no reason for being apart from fulfilling an assignment (whether it's a first-year required research paper or a required doctoral dissertation—in many cases still the most narrowly conceived kind of academic writing). We need to make research exciting, interesting for both the researcher and the audience, and tailored in terms of methods of inquiry, subject matter, and the researcher's goals.

To that end, in the first-year writing class, I assign students a range of activities that help them understand the role primary research plays in their own work, just as I do in the advanced courses. Good pedagogy is good pedagogy, regardless of the level of instruction. The research and writing ideas presented in this chapter are engaging for students at every level, seen most clearly at the end-of-the-semester mini-conferences I organize every term. Students formally present their work, usually in a space outside the classroom, to fellow students and invited guests, many of whom are participants in their research studies. Students take ownership of their projects, creating Prezis, PowerPoints, posterboards, and videos in sharing their findings. The concluding class event is an academic conference, and the students know that they are scholars.

Works Cited

Buehl, Jonathan, Tamar Chute, and Anne Fields. "Training in the Archives: Archival Research as Professional Development." *College Composition and Communication*, vol. 64, no. 2, 2012, pp. 274–305.

Donahue, Patricia, and Gretchen Flesher Moon, eds. *Local Histories: Reading the Archives of Composition*. University of Pittsburgh Press, 2007.

Gaillet, Lynée Lewis, and Michelle Eble. *Primary Research and Writing: People, Places, and Spaces*. Routledge, 2015.

Glenn, Cheryl, and Jessica Enoch. "Drama in the Archives: Rereading Methods, Rewriting History." *College Composition and Communication*, vol. 61, no. 2, December 2009.

Hayden, Wendy. " 'Gifts' of the Archives: A Pedagogy for Undergraduate Research." *College Composition and Communication*, vol. 66, no. 3, 2015, pp. 402–426.

Kimbell, Emily. E-mail to the author. 9 February 2017.

Kirsch, Gesa E., and Liz Rohan, editors. *Beyond the Archives: Research as a Lived Process*. Southern Illinois University Press, 2008.

Ramsey, Alexis, Wendy Sharer, Barbara L'Eplattenier, and Lisa Mastrangelo, eds. *Working in the Archives: Practical Research Methods in Rhetoric and Composition*. Southern Illinois University Press, 2010.

Rose, Jessica. E-mail to the author. 8 February 2017.

Ryan, Mandy. E-mail to the author. 11 February 2017.

Shamoon, Linda K., et al. *Coming of Age: The Advanced Writing Curriculum*. Heinemann Boynton/Cook, 2002.

Chapter 14. Composing Communities: Blogs as Learning Communities in the First-Year Composition Classroom

Kathryn Crowther

PERIMETER COLLEGE AT GEORGIA STATE UNIVERSITY

Writing is only one of the many things that happen in the freshman writing classroom. As the name implies, the focus of a *first-year composition* course (FYC) could be seen as resting equally on the *first-year* or *freshman* component of the course title. Granted, not all students in a FYC class are actually first-year college students, but the name implies that there is an element of initiation, of learning something related to maturity and experience, as well as the more obvious sense of an *introductory* writing class. Indeed, as we work with students to practice and improve their writing, it becomes clear that there is so much more to learning how to write than just writing. Besides the more obvious pedagogical objectives embedded in a writing class (reading comprehension, critical thinking, argument development, drafting, revising, etc.), there are the arguably more valuable learning habits and life skills that are inextricably tied to the writing process. In the first-year writing classroom, students develop the routines and attitudes that will shape their approach to writing and to learning throughout their college and future careers; it is, therefore, our job as writing teachers to connect the acquisition of those skills to the learning objectives of the composition course.

When I teach first-year writing, I am also teaching time management, note-taking, brainstorming, process, revising, and other learning strategies that help students perceive writing as an organic, integral part of their personal and professional development. Of course, the primary objective of a FYC course is to have our students practice and improve their writing skills through a variety of writing assignments. There is a significant body of work on the benefits of using *low-stakes* writing in the composition classroom (see Elbow's essay, "High Stakes and Low Stakes in Assigning and Responding to Writing"); for regular low-stakes writing, I have found that blogs work well to give students a personal space to develop their writing skills. In my freshman composition classroom, blogs serve as a place for brainstorming, drafting, thinking through arguments, considering audience, and reflecting on our reading and class discussion; in short, we use the blog to work through all the steps of the writing process. But as I've used blogs as an integral part of my writing courses, I've noticed that the blogs come to serve a different purpose, one that is perhaps more beneficial to the students as a whole than my overt pedagogical goals. The more the students blog, the more they develop a strong sense of their writing self, and the more they lay claim to their individual writing persona and develop strong writing habits. Yet commensurately, they become part of a larger blogging community, and they begin to exchange dialog with their peers and with external readers in a way that gives their writing a sense of authenticity and purpose in the real world. Blogging, therefore, expands the boundaries of the classroom and creates an authentic community that benefits the students in both the development of their writing and learning skills and in their sense of participation in larger, higher-stakes learning community that stretches beyond our classroom.

I have asked my students to reflect upon the role that blogging has had on their writing and on their experience of the class, and I have asked them to participate in surveys and focus groups to gauge how students evaluate the role of blogging in our classroom. In 70 student blog post reflections, 50 final evaluations, and three *focus group* sessions, students overwhelmingly responded that while they found weekly blogging a chore, it benefited both their writing and their sense of participation and community in the class.

Blogs (short for *Weblogs*) provide an online venue for individual writing as well as a forum for interactive communication through the *comment* function. Teachers of writing and communication have recognized the value of such a space and blogs are now increasingly common in the composition classroom. Overwhelmingly, the literature on blogs in the classroom suggests both their potential as writing forums and their ability to house multi-modal forms of communication. An overview of blogs being used in the composition classroom by Steven Krause "suggest[s] that many writing teachers seem to be using blog spaces as places to facilitate dynamic and interactive writing experiences." (Will Richardson writes, for example, "Blogs are being used as class portals, online filing cabinets for student work, e-portfolios, collaborative space, knowledge management, and even school websites" [21].) In "Writing and Citizenship: Using Blogs to Teach First-Year Composition," Charles Tryon details his use of blogs in several composition courses. Tryon argues that blogging works as a composition tool as it encourages a "no-holds barred argumentative style" (128) and provides an informal way for students to reference their own writing in class discussion.

Much of the emphasis in critical discussions of blogging is placed on the notion of space. As Ferdig and Trammell write in "Content Delivery in the 'Blogosphere'":

> Blogs are useful teaching and learning tools because they provide a space for students to reflect and publish their thoughts and understandings.... Blogs also feature hyperlinks, which help students begin to understand the relational and contextual basis of knowledge, knowledge construction and meaning making.

The space that blogs provide, the critics argue, is both personal and public, allowing for meditative writing along with interactive linking and collaborative commenting. Furthermore, as much of the literature observes, blogging encourages students to consider audience in a more dynamic way than they do with a standard academic essay. The idea that a post will be open for readers to comment on and give immediate feedback changes the notion of writing as static and final to dynamic and evolving. As Will Richardson writes, "ultimately, [a] post is still a draft, a way to test my best ideas and writing against an audience" (31). To summarize in Richardson's words: "The differences between blogging in this manner and writing as we traditionally think of it are clear: Writing stops; blogging continues. Writing is inside; blogging is outside. Writing is monologue; blogging is conversation. Writing is thesis; blogging is synthesis" (31). In contrast to other online writing mediums such as Twitter, blogs provide a more customizable and open-ended writing space, a place students can go to write drafts, continuously edit and refine posts, add pictures, and, perhaps most importantly, face a blank page that forces them to rehearse their writing personae. When students practice writing in a low-stakes environment that is designed for frequent writing, reader interaction, and limitless chances to edit, they grow comfortable with a flexible writing process that encourages drafting, feedback, and revision.

I have employed blogs in my composition classes for several years with varying degrees of success. I originally began assigning blogs as a more dynamic space for students to keep a weekly writing journal but quickly found that it was also useful as a space for pre-writing exercises; in fact, I now use blogs for all phases of the writing process from free-writing, clustering, outlining, to drafting and editing. After experimenting with different models, I settled on the *hub-and-spoke* style of blogging in which each student keeps a personal blog, but they are all connected to a central class blog that I run. (When I designed my course blog, I used the model described by Boone B. Gorges at teleogistic.net/2009/08/hub-and-spoke-blogging-with-lots-of-students/.) At the beginning of the semester, I help the students set up their own WordPress blogs (these can be hosted independently at wordpress.com or hosted on a school server) and I introduce the blogging assignment, explaining to students that they are required to keep the blog all semester and write a minimum of one substantial post (150–300 words) per week on a topic related to class. However, I stress that they are encouraged to blog much more than that, to blog about other things loosely related to our course (though I discourage *diary* type blogging) or to link to relevant media content. I also encourage them to personalize their blogs, to choose a new template and to add links, pictures, videos, and other media to make the blog space individual and multi-modal. Typically, about 75% of the class follows these recommendations, while 25% of the students do the minimum weekly post and do not personalize their blog. All students are put into *blog groups* with four or five of their classmates and are responsible for reading and commenting on their group members' posts weekly; I do this both to make the reading-load manageable and to create small blogging communities. These individual student blogs form the spokes and I run a central *hub* blog that works to connect them. As I often teach multiple sections of the same course, it is useful to create one hub and then have all the different sections link from that hub; that way, the students in the different sections can communicate with each other and share in conversations that stretch outside of their class and into others. On my central blog I do my own blogging as a way to model good writing, and I also pull exemplary posts from students to the front page in a weekly "blog post of the week"—again, this serves to model good writing and to bring interesting or provocative topics to the forefront. I'll talk more about the way that this model builds community later in this essay, but first I'll address the benefits of individual blogging.

Blogs provide several advantages as a writing tool in comparison to word-processors or pen-and-paper composition. First of all, they provide a space which can be modified and personalized by the students, encouraging them to make an investment in their writing space. Similarly, blogging promotes student awareness of the different media available for writing and how the design and organization of that space can influence their creativity and ownership of their ideas. Many students wrote in their reflections that they enjoyed personalizing their blogs and felt more invested in their writing and participating in the class as a result. As the student comments show, the idea that the blog is not only a space for work but also a place for creativity and individuality seems to open up students to investing in the writing process and feeling proud of owning their writing space. I find this has a much more powerful effect than writing on a word processor or in a generic notebook.

Figure 14.1. Sample student blog posts using creative visual design.

Initially, I find that students are resistant to blogging. Despite the invitation to blog as often as they want, most students limit themselves to the weekly required posts and blog primarily about the class reading. This kind of blogging has its own advantages: first of all, it pushes the students to think more deeply about the reading, rather than skimming it before class. As a result, students come to class having processed the ideas and contribute to our discussion more readily; indeed, many of the comments in my class begin with "I blogged about this and. . . . " I often ask students to have their blogs open in class so they can remind themselves of their impressions of the text we are discussing—in this way the blogs serve as a space for pre-writing and critical thinking. Additionally, reading their peers' blogs allows the students to see the different ways people can read and react to a text and better prepares them for the multiplicity of opinions and readings they encounter in our class discussion. Reading another student's reaction to a text often causes students to rethink their own position and results in a deeper reflection on the more complex elements of the reading.

Figure 14.2. Blogging about the challenging topic of disability.

This deeper engagement with the reading leads to the second advantage I observe with the blog platform: the development of more sophisticated critical thinking skills. In the spring semester of 2012 I organized my composition course around a difficult and often controversial topic: disability. At the onset of the course, many students expressed their anxiety (and reluctance) to talk about a topic that was fraught with political correctness and—as many claimed—was outside of the realm of their experience. As students tackled some difficult theoretical readings, the blogs became a space to explore the complexities of the topic and the ways to talk about a difficult subject. The more we read and discussed in class, the more the students began to *talk out* their apprehension in their blog, and many wrote candidly about how they had seen their awareness and understanding of the complexities of the rhetoric of disability transform as they had read and discussed our texts. This level of critical engagement was augmented,

I firmly believe, by the nature of blogging—both confessional and public. (For a detailed discussion of the productive public/private dynamic of the academic blog, see Fernheimer and Nelson.)

After the first few weeks, I find that the handful of students who move past the weekly blog assignment and use the blog as a personal writing space (these students are often already familiar with the genre of blogging) begin to inspire other students to branch out in their blogging. More and more, students write posts about other aspects of the course and, in many cases, about their broader experience as college students. This movement towards spontaneous, self-generated content pushes students to think more about the act of writing and brings, I would argue, some of the greatest benefits in both academic skills and writing skills. Many students commented in their final reflections that at the beginning of the semester it was a chore to sit down and think of something to write about. However, as the semester progressed, they found that they began to think about their blog as they went through their day and made mental notes to write about their experiences later. With our focus on rhetoric and communication, students began to see the quotidian arguments that surround them and posts on Super Bowl advertising, election rhetoric, and campus controversies began to appear on their blogs. Other aspects of the blog format benefit the students' writing skills. The chronology of the blog format (entries generally appear in reverse chronological order with the most recent entry appearing first) helps them to conceptualize the process of writing an academic paper as a multiple-step process that evolves over time, with plenty of time for revision and editing. I frequently asked students to begin thinking through a topic with a free-write or brainstorm on their blog and then begin shaping those raw ideas into more structured essays. As this comment shows, many students expressed that beginning a writing assignment was much easier and less stressful when they had blogged about it first.

Indeed, the more the students write, the more comfortable they feel writing, and many of them begin to post regularly and to fill their blog space with personalized content. Perhaps the most common (and most rewarding) comment that students made in their evaluations was that the act of sitting down to write became easier as the semester progressed. Many wrote that what was so challenging at the beginning of the semester—finding time to write, coming up with a topic, organizing ideas, starting to write on the blank screen, meeting the word count for the post—grew gradually easier the more they wrote. As they took ownership of their site, they became more confident with their writing and began branching out to new topics and engaging with other media, embedding videos, linking to external content and to other students' blogs. In this way, students *rehearsed* their writing personae in the way that Pamela Henney suggests in her chapter in this volume on "Acting the Author." By acting the role of the academic author in a low-stakes (and, therefore, low-anxiety) setting, students ultimately blossomed as writers and as individuals, finding and claiming their voice and their right to speak in the strange mix of public and private that constitutes a blog.

As they become confident individual writers, a sense of community grows up around the blogs. The dual nature of blogs—that they foster individual writing and yet create a network of interconnected readers and writers—distinguishes blog writing from journaling or weekly response papers. The potential for a self-sustaining (and to some degree, self-governing) community to emerge organically from a blog network is exciting for teachers of all subjects and it effectively flips control and management of the assignment and the larger dynamics of the class over to the students. One of the first critical writers on the genre of weblogging, Rebecca Blood imagined the benefits of the blog community as a place where a writer would feel comfortable expressing opinions in a public venue:

> As he enunciates his opinions daily, this new awareness of his inner life may develop into a trust in his own perspective. His own reactions—to a poem, to other people, and, yes, to the media—will carry more weight with him. Accustomed to expressing his thoughts on his website, he will be able to more fully articulate his opinions to himself and others. He will become impatient with waiting to see what others think before he decides, and will begin to act in accordance with his inner voice instead. Ideally, he will become less reflexive and more reflective, and find his own opinions and ideas worthy of serious consideration.

In my course, the sense of community begins within the small blogging groups but generally grows to include the whole class and, by the end of the semester, all three of my sections. What starts out as a requirement to read their group members' weekly posts and leave a comment becomes an ongoing conversation that takes place both in and out of the classroom. As I read the students' blogs, I see that discussions that we began in class are continuing and evolving in their blog posts and in the comments, and vice versa: conversations that begin on the blogs come into class discussion and allow the students to shape and guide where our exploration of a topic goes. Again, there is an evolution in confidence and voice that I see over the course of the semester; while initial comments are perfunctory and nearly always complimentary ("Great post!"), by the mid-point of the semester students are really responding to each other and providing feedback and counterpoints.

The blog comments provide another vital element of the writing process: authentic audience and feedback. Rather than writing solely for the teacher, students know that their peers are reading their posts and it raises the stakes of the exercise in a more authentic way than grading. Occasionally outside readers find the blogs and leave comments, which both exhilarates and scares students when they realize that their public voice is finding an audience! Additionally, when their peers leave feedback on their writing, it reinforces and augments the classroom peer review in a more informal setting. The same students who question their authority to give feedback to their peers early in the semester, often leave honest and constructive critique on their group members' writing later in the year. The blogs help to showcase that writing is a collaborative, reader-focused endeavor, and an ongoing community in which they are all always both writer and audience.

At the *hub* of the class blogs is the centralized blog that I use for several purposes. First, at the beginning of the semester, I blog along with the students to showcase how the blogging genre works (writing with embedded media and links) and to model good writing. In this way, the blog serves as the kind of holistic space that Rachel Anya Dearie Fomalhaut describes in her essay on affective pedagogy in this volume. After watching as I demonstrate writing a blog post in class, students can then go home and practice the physical and mental process of writing, including dealing with the difficulties of getting started, finding the right voice, deleting and re-writing, and dealing with frustration and writer's block. I can model how to deal with these normal yet typically unaddressed writing challenges and help students work through them.

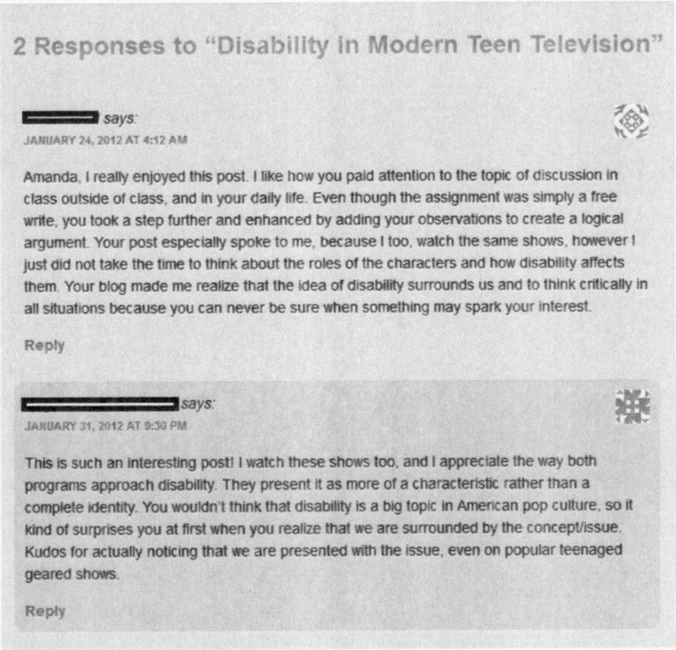

Figure 14.3. Reader dialog and feedback in the comments.

Second, I use the class blog as a place to bring attention to exemplary writing and to the innovative, creative blogging that some students are doing. Each week I solicit nominations from students for the best blog posts they've read that week. I then choose the best post from each section and post it to the central blog along with a short commentary on what made it an exemplary post; in this way, I can spotlight specific writing issues as well as discuss general writing strategies and highlight what topics are circulating in the class. The winners of "Blog Post of the Week" (BPOTW) receive bonus participation points and it becomes a coveted award. At the mid-point of the semester, I hand BPOTW over to volunteers who *guest-host* it for extra credit. Although this began as a time-saving strategy on my part, I found that turning the evaluation process over to the students leads to a more sophisticated type of peer review and slightly higher stakes for the blogging assignment.

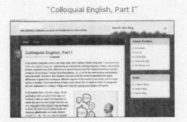

Guest Blog Post of the Week

October 31, 2011 in Uncategorized

Hello, class! This week I am guest hosting Blog Post of the Week! And the winners are....

"There's No Place Like Home"

's post about how venturing into other cultures makes her appreciate her own culture more is both a continuation of her previous post "The World, at our Fingertips" and an answer to   's post challenging her argument. I think she makes accurate points about the importance of exploring foreign cultures and supports her belief that the the cultures of the world should be explored excellently. I love that Allison and Robert are using their blogs as a medium for debate!

"Colloquial English, Part I"

Figure 14.4. Student guest-hosting blog post of the week.

The learning community that evolves as a result of the blogs has surprised me each semester in the way that it strengthens and improves *all* aspects of the course and of the students' engagement. Most obviously, the regular writing and the authentic audience with peer-review that the comments provide lead to better writing in general, and the interactive blog medium pushes students to think about the ways that writing is collaborative and multi-modal. But, more importantly, as the students blog and read their peers' blogs, the ongoing discussions that the blog engenders unite the class in a mutual conversation about our topic and a collaborative endeavor to practice and improve our communication skills. Students comment that they feel like they get to know their classmates better through the blogs, and, over the course of the semester, more students share personal experiences on their blogs which spill over into our discussions about being a college student; managing work-loads; prioritizing academic work, mental and physical health, relationships; and other topics that connect back to the general *life* skills the class is building. Overall, camaraderie develops that exceeds the requirements of the course and turns the class into a community. While this is advantageous in simply making class a more fun place to be, the benefits of a learning community are closely linked to student engagement and the achievement of the learning objectives of the course. (For more on the connection between learning communities and student engagement, see Barkley [25].) Ironically, the lower-stakes environment of the blog creates a higher-stakes community to which the students are motivated to contribute. And students who feel that more is at stake in the course than simply showing up and turning in assignments ultimately produce stronger work and are more likely to generalize and transfer the skills they have acquired.

Of course, as with any assignment, there are problems and pitfalls associated with using blogs in the classroom. Not all students commit to the assignment, and their blogs wither early in the semester. Some students use the blogs inappropriately as a personal journal, and I have to monitor them carefully to ensure that inappropriate content isn't shared. I give my students the option of making their blogs private, but the majority choose to have them open on the web which raises privacy and copyright issues (though I do use the former to have important discussions about the ramifications of personal disclosure on the public web and the latter to hammer home the rules of copyright, attribution, and citation as it regards digital publication). And of course, despite the preponderance of positive comments about the value of the blogging assignment, nearly all students complain that weekly blogging is too much and they find it hard to keep up with. Some also complain that being forced to blog contradicts the spirit of the blogging genre, a comment which points to the central weakness of the blogging assignment: that *real* communities rise up and sustain themselves organically, whereas a forced community will always fail in some fundamental ways. In his essay, "When Blogging Goes Bad: A Cautionary Tale About Blogs, Email Lists, Discussion, and Interaction," Steven Krause discusses how his use of blogs in the college classroom floundered when students failed to post frequently and used the blog only to answer the assigned discussion prompts. Rather than becoming a dynamic writing space, then, the blogs became yet another assignment to be completed in rote fashion. As Krause acknowledges, Jill Walker's question, "How empowering is it to be forced to blog?" highlights the contradictory impulse of assigning blog entries as short essay responses while hoping that students will feel empowered to take control of their own writing space. Yet, all in all, I have found the blogs to be an overwhelmingly positive component in the first-year writing classroom, specifically in their capacity to bring central issues about writing and collegiate experience to the foreground and to reinforce good writing and study habits. As individuals, students hone their writing skills and learn to consider audience and to give critique and feedback. As a class, the blog network creates a communal space that extends the confines of the classroom and brings students together in a common endeavor. And as the community of blogging students grows, the class becomes the decentralized, self-motivating, and self-critiquing classroom we are striving to achieve.

Works Cited

Barkley, Elizabeth. *Student Engagement Techniques: A Handbook for College Faculty.* Jossey-Bass, 2010.

Blood, Rebecca. "Weblogs: A history and perspective." *Rebecca's Pocket,* 7 September 2000. www.rebeccablood.net/essays/weblog_history.html.

Elbow, Peter. "High Stakes and Low Stakes in Assigning and Responding to Writing." *Assigning and Responding to Writing in the Disciplines,* edited by Mary Deane Sorcinelli and Peter Elbow. Jossey-Bass, 1997.

Ferdig, Richard E., and Kaye D. Trammell. "Content Delivery in the 'Blogosphere.'" *T.H.E. Journal,* February 2004.

Fernheimer, Janice Wendi, and Thomas J. Nelson. "Bridging the Composition Divide: Blog Pedagogy and the Potential for Agonistic Classrooms." *Currents in Electronic Literacy,* no. 9, Fall 2005.

Krause, Steven D. "When Blogging Goes Bad: A Cautionary Tale About Blogs, Email Lists, Discussion, and Interaction." *Kairos,* vol. 9, no. 1, September 2004.

Richardson, Will. *Blogs, Wikis, Podcasts, and Other Powerful Web Tools for Classrooms.* Corwin Press, 2006.

Tryon, Charles. "Writing and Citizenship: Using Blogs to Teach First-Year Composition." *Pedagogy,* vol. 6, no. 1, Winter 2006, pp. 128–132.

Chapter 15. Promoting Academic Skills through Writing: "The Survey of Academic Skills Essay" Assignment

Lisa Whalen
NORTH HENNEPIN COMMUNITY COLLEGE

The number of students arriving at college unprepared to complete college-level work has increased significantly during the past decades. In fall 2000, the U.S. Department of Education found that 42% of first-year students at public two-year colleges and 20% of first-year students at public four-year colleges required at least one remedial course before they were ready to enroll in college-level courses. By 2009, an ACT National Curriculum Survey found that only 26% of professors thought new college students were prepared for college-level assignments (5). Although students and faculty sometimes differ in how they define college readiness, these studies indicate that in addition to entering college without necessary content-area knowledge, many students lack basic academic skills, such as knowing how to study, manage time, prioritize, and communicate appropriately. These skills also happen to be in high demand but short supply across many of the job markets for which colleges are preparing graduates, according to a national survey of business and nonprofit leaders (Hart Associates). As a result, college faculty face a dilemma: Do we help students succeed by *stealing* time from course content to teach academic skills, or do we cover content thoroughly but risk leaving behind students who haven't mastered academic skills? How can we help students understand the value of such skills, not only for college, but for employment and civic engagement as well? Fortunately, composition instructors are in a unique position to teach both content and academic skills without shortchanging either. The Survey of Academic Skills Essay, which can be applied to developmental or first-year writing courses, allows instructors to reinforce academic skills while also teaching academic writing. It implements intentional learning by asking students to become more self-aware of their academic strengths and weaknesses in order to plot a course to build on strengths and improve weaknesses. Through integrative learning, students apply the skills they are learning as part of the writing preparation and composition process.

Process and Product: An Overview of the Survey of Academic Skills Essay

Instructors disagree about whether composition courses should emphasize product or process, but some assignments highlight both. Although the Survey of

Academic Skills Essay (SASE) assignment is product-driven in that it asks students to submit an essay for grading, it emphasizes process by breaking the essay into a series of steps that illustrate the writing process. Like writing assignments students complete in many college courses, the SASE teaches time management skills that instructors want students to develop and that employers seek when hiring by requiring students to meet short-term deadlines while remaining focused on the long-term goal of turning in a polished essay (Maguire).

Step One: Defining Success

Step one of SASE launches the brainstorming stage of the writing process, introduces prioritizing, and reinforces time management. Students begin the assignment by responding in writing to the prompt "Define what it means to be a successful college student." To prevent automatic responses, such as "Get As in my classes" or "Do the homework," instructors can ask students to make lists of their short- and long-term goals, challenges they face in achieving their goals, and time they spend each week on other commitments, like jobs and family care. From this exercise, students generate personalized definitions of success based on realistic expectations. For example, to some, being a successful college student means balancing work, school, and family. To others, success in college means maintaining a particular GPA, being accepted into a program/major, or participating in as many campus activities as possible while still passing their classes.

Step Two: Developing a Survey

Step two of SASE introduces audience awareness and information-gathering in addition to the academic skills of self-presentation, communicating with peers, and receiving feedback. Each student creates a survey about becoming a successful college student, which he/she distributes to 10 people who are not members of our class. I provide a list of sample survey questions, for instance, *What resources (writing center, tutoring, study groups, etc.) do you find helpful?* and *What strategies do you use to avoid procrastinating?* Up to three questions on each student's survey may come from my list. Students must generate the remaining questions, for a total of five. Deciding what they want to learn from the survey encourages students to think about their strengths and weaknesses as learners and increases their investment in the assignment. Creating and distributing the surveys also teaches students to handle the specific time management challenges that arise while working with others because the longer they wait to create and distribute their surveys, the less time respondents have to complete and return them, which decreases students' ability to meet deadlines for the next steps in the assignment.

Developing these surveys also provides a brief introduction to the in-depth primary research students will be required to perform for future assignments, like the one described by Lynee Lewis Gaillet in "Primary Research in the

Undergraduate Writing Classroom." Exposure to primary research on a small scale allows students to discover the types of problems that can crop up and how to contend with them before beginning a higher-stakes research project, such as in a capstone project for their major, later on.

Students submit their surveys and a plan for distribution (e.g. via email, Surveymonkey, social media, or face-to-face conversation) to me. While requiring my approval may dampen students' ownership of their research, it provides two important benefits: it helps ensure survey questions will elicit useful responses, thereby sparking discussions focused on audience awareness, and it demonstrates how ongoing feedback and revision are integral to the writing process. For example, I emphasize audience awareness by pointing out how people outside of our class might be unfamiliar with the phrase "academic skills" and therefore unsure how to answer a question like "How can someone improve their academic skills?" I ask students who plan to distribute surveys via SurveyMonkey (a free tool for designing online surveys) if their respondents are likely to have enough computer literacy to answer questions online. I suggest surveys comprised of open-ended questions may be more effective if conducted online instead of face-to-face because respondents will have more time to think about their answers. In some cases, I recommend changing open-ended questions to multiple choice in order to produce analyzable data. In addition to changing their surveys to accommodate respondents' needs, students develop audience awareness by considering which responses will be most beneficial for their audience and therefore worth including in their essays.

As students distribute their surveys, they practice self-presentation. In a culture where consumers are regularly asked to complete surveys by restaurants, department stores, and repair shops, they have to figure out how to present themselves as serious scholars conducting worthwhile research so respondents will provide thoughtful answers. If students aren't getting any responses to their surveys, we talk about why that is and how they can increase the response rate.

Step Three: Analyzing Survey Responses

Step three ushers students into the planning stage of the writing process and teaches analysis and prioritization. I provide a chart (see Figure 15.1) with sample survey questions and responses that students complete by plugging in their survey results.

Students use their completed charts to analyze responses and then write a summary of what they learn. Writing the summary encourages students to prioritize by selecting only the most important ideas from the information they gathered, and then to state those ideas clearly and concisely in their own words. In college-level or research-based composition courses, I add a requirement: Students must find one or more outside sources and compare and contrast what the source(s) says about academic skills to their survey responses. Depending on course goals and time constraints, I may also include lessons on locating sources and evaluating their credibility or change the essay from exploratory/reflective to argumentative.

Name of person who completed survey (or, if you don't want to use names, give each person a number)	Survey Question 1: How do you avoid procrastinating?	Survey Question 2: How do you study for exams?	Survey Question 3:	Survey Question 4:	Survey Question 5:
Pat	Write assignment due dates in the calendar on my iphone.	Use a free, online program to make flashcards			
Jim	List each day's homework in the planner I was given during the first week of classes.	Take notes on all readings and lectures. Review my notes with a study group before the exam.			

Figure 15.1: Sample Survey Response Chart

In addition to helping students generate ideas for their essays, the summary serves as a first step in planning how they will present their research to readers. I read and respond—either orally or in writing—to each student's summary and provide suggestions for turning the summary into an essay, which reinforces audience awareness, self-presentation, and the *looping* nature of receiving feedback and revising. It also prepares students for a workforce in which "employers are unequivocally telling [researchers] that they want graduates who can translate technical expertise and complex data into cogent, meaningful and persuasive arguments" (Maguire). Students practice these skills by deciding how best to use their data to develop and support thesis statements both before and during the drafting process.

Step Four: Writing a Rough Draft

Step four moves students into the drafting stage of the writing process and teaches them how to apply what they've learned. Application is particularly important for both retaining knowledge and succeeding in the job market. A 2013 survey of employers by Hart found that "applied knowledge, written and oral communication," and the ability to "conduct research and use evidence-based analysis" were among five key areas employers wanted colleges to emphasize. This assignment addresses each of those, particularly by asking students to reflect on and analyze what they've learned by responding to the following questions in their essay drafts:

- How do you define what it means to be a successful college student?
- What past experiences (good and bad) have shaped who you are as a student? as a writer?
- What did you think academic skills were before you began working on this assignment?
- What have you learned about academic skills from working on this assignment?
- What is/are the most useful thing(s) you've learned from this assignment?
- How can you use what you've learned about academic skills to become a successful college student?

By reflecting on past experiences, assessing current skills, and thinking about how they can apply what they've learned to form future habits, students begin forming, as Kathryn Crowther describes in her essay for this volume, "the routines and attitudes that will shape their approach to writing and to learning throughout their college and future careers." The earlier they form these routines and attitudes, the more integral those routines become to students' identities as successful college students.

Step Five: Using Feedback to Revise

Step five reintroduces the feedback-revising loop, this time as an *official* stage of the writing process. Through peer review, students learn to give and receive feedback, something they'll need to do in almost every aspect of their personal and professional lives. Many do not feel confident enough in their own writing skill to critique someone else's, and there is always a risk that students will give misguided advice. Still, I include peer review in the SASE assignment because it exposes them to the idea that there are many different ways to craft an essay from a single assignment. According to the National Capital Research Council, instructors can reduce the likelihood that students will provide misguided advice during peer review by establishing clear guidelines. Therefore, my students and I co-create a peer review checklist. A typical checklist includes the following:

- Identify the writer's thesis.
- Does it make a claim?
- Does it forecast the essay's main ideas?
- How could the claim and/or main ideas be stated more clearly?
- Examine each paragraph and identify topic sentence(s), supporting details, and transitions. If one of these is missing, indicate which one and where it is missing.
- Give at least one suggestion as to how the introduction could better grab readers' attention.
- Give at least one suggestion as to how the writer could make the conclusion more dynamic.
- Note any sentences that are unclear. What about them could be clearer?

I also impose a fairly standard structure on how peer review is conducted. The structure asks students to read their work aloud in small groups and discuss responses to the questions for each essay. A unique benefit of peer review for this assignment is that by reading peers' drafts, students teach each other what they've learned about academic skills, such as how to study for exams or what resources the college provides. Sharing feedback and knowledge of college resources is key to students' success. In fact, studies show that "students who talk about substantive matters with faculty and peers . . . and receive frequent feedback on their performance typically get better grades, are more satisfied with college, and are more likely to persist [in college]" (Kuh). The link between social interaction and persistence is particularly strong for underprepared students (Kuh).

Separate from peer review, I provide written comments and, depending on time constraints, schedule one-on-one conferences to discuss students' drafts. Students are required to schedule the conference in advance, show up on time, and bring questions about their drafts, thereby practicing time management and self-presentation. Lastly, I encourage students to seek additional feedback by offering a chance to increase their final essay score by half a letter grade (e.g. B to B+) if they submit a signed form showing they met with a Writing Center tutor. After peer review and conferences, students use all of the feedback they have received to revise their rough drafts.

Step Six: Presenting Survey Results

If time permits, students present their survey results to the class. Presenters must make their research clear and interesting for their audience, occasionally incorporating charts, graphs, or other audio/visual elements, which requires additional reflection on their data and audience needs. Members of peer review groups provide moral support for the nervous and lead the applause once a presentation is over, thereby strengthening social relationships. Presenters and audience members discover they can learn from one another, which is a revelation to many. As Gaillet points out in her essay in this volume, primary research allows students to "become the experts on topics in which they are vested." Seeing themselves as experts on academic skills helps them develop confidence in their ability to become successful college students and to offer support to peers.

Step Seven: Submitting a Final Draft

Preparing to submit a final draft includes editing and proofreading, though how much time we spend on them depends on time constraints. Students assess the strengths and weaknesses of their essays and consider one last time how to best present what they have learned to their audience. Then, I give students feedback in the form of a detailed grading rubric.

Feedback from Students: Reflections on the Assignment

According to students' essays and comments on course evaluations, this assignment has been successful in teaching a range of writing, academic, and life skills. Most comments fall into one of three categories: discovery of new resources, increased awareness of habits, and improved writing.

Several students indicated that as a result of this assignment they began using campus resources such as the Writing Center, the Advising Office, and the Career Services Center for the first time—an improvement over 2013 CCSSE (Community

College Survey of Student Engagement) results for NHCC that indicated although 75% of students surveyed rated tutoring services as "somewhat important" or "very important," only 27% reported using those services. Responses for financial aid advising, transfer credit assistance, academic advising, and career planning ranged from 78–90% of students rating them important but only 15–55% of students using them (Olson 14). Data indicates students don't use the services unless given a good reason because so much of their time outside of class is taken up by work and family responsibilities. However, if convinced by a source they trust—a peer—that a college service is beneficial, they make time to use it (Olson 12–14).

In analyzing responses to her survey about studying for exams, one student noted, "I was surprised how many people use study groups. It seems like a smart and helpful resource." Another student summarized the links between devising a survey question, analyzing responses to it, and applying what she learned from the responses—a mirror of both learning and writing processes:

> I wanted to know specifically what strategies are used to avoid falling behind on homework or in a class. . . . [S]ixty percent [of respondents] said that they spread [the work] out or put Post-It notes all over to remind them, forty percent said that they just do it, ten percent said that if they are having problems they will go to a tutor to get help. I found this very helpful and plan to go to the writing center for some assistance in writing a stronger paper.

Students' comments about their own writing reflected increases in audience awareness and willingness to invest time in the writing process. One such comment explained, "I cannot stress the importance of brainstorming, proofreading and acknowledging your target audience. Before this assignment I lacked the understanding of these three skills in writing. I now understand that every writing needs to have effective ideas and an understanding of the target audience."

Some of the most insightful comments described students' increasing awareness of their habits and of the relationship between habits and success. A student whose survey focused on organization summarized her results this way: "[My respondents use] a planner. Many of them put their class times down, when they will study and do homework, when everything is due and when tests are. I truly believe by staying organized helps you to become a better student." Another student discovered links between motivation, habits, and success:

> . . . [O]ne of my participants said she prepares for class by mentally motivating herself to be ready for whatever she will be learning that day. . . . [Now] I mentally motivate myself by thinking of the life I'm going to have after I graduate. I know in order to graduate, I need to get good grades and actively participate [in class].

These comments also ranged from a narrow focus on one habit to the nature of habits in general. Regarding her time management habits, a student wrote, "One of the first problems that needed to be changed was my inability to manage time effectively. . . . It's amazing how prioritizing my life had such significance. I started getting better grades in school and my overall stress level was reduced. . . ." A second student described her learning process:

> Prior to developing the survey and learning study habits of others, I thought academic skills were how smart one was. . . . After developing the survey and reading the responses from individuals, I now understand that academic skills refer to much more. . . . Academic skills refer to habits and practices that the student has in preparation for each task handed out by the instructor.

Conclusion

Perhaps the most important thing I've learned from this assignment is that when students perceive a direct link between what they are learning and how it will benefit them, they are more likely to become invested in their education and to take ownership of their learning. That, after all, is the aim of integrative learning. As an added bonus, my investment in students' learning increases along with theirs. The essays document students' growth as human beings in ways that both they and I find rewarding.

Works Cited

ACT National Curriculum Survey 2009. *ACT,* 2009. www.act.org/research/policy makers/pdf/NationalCurriculumSurvey2009.pdf.

Hart Research Associates. "It Takes More than a Major: Employer Priorities for College Learning and Student Success: Overview and Key Findings." *Association of American Colleges & Universities,* 10 April 2013. aacu.org/sites/default/files/files /LEAP/2013_EmployerSurvey.pdf.

Kuh, George, D. "What Student Engagement Data Tells Us about College Readiness: Student Preparation, Motivation, and Achievement." *Association of American Colleges & Universities,* 2007. www.aacu.org/publications-research/periodicals /what-student-engagement-data-tell-us-about-college-readiness.

Maguire Associates. "Employers Rate Internships and Work Experience as Most Important Criteria for Hiring College Graduates; Although Deeper Look Shows How Much They Still Value Liberal Arts Outcomes." *Insights for a Changing Economy,* vol. 4, no. 1, 2014.

Olson, Sheryl. "Overview of the 2013 CCSSE Survey Results." Office of Institutional Effectiveness, North Hennepin Community College, 2013.

Chapter 16. My Composition or Yours? What We Teach in First-Year Composition

Abigail G. Scheg

WESTERN GOVERNORS UNIVERSITY

Students filter through the academic system at the two year college at a rapid pace and it is difficult for me, as a writing instructor, to envision a consistent, effective pedagogical strategy. Each semester of General Education classes—like Research Writing, College Writing, Introduction to Literature, or Basic Writing— the student population seems to balloon with one specific major. For instance, one College Writing class was almost entirely nursing students, whereas a Basic Writing course was mostly Special Education majors. These unique microcosms break down the greater question of "What should I teach in first-year composition?" to a particular dichotomy: my composition or yours?

Nursing students will use a unique blend of Latin, English, and acronyms in their daily career writing to assess charts, prescriptions, and translate doctors' handwriting. Though this is a necessary skill for nursing students to possess, it would seem out of context to rely on the composition instructor to teach these skills. However, it also seems inappropriate to have these students compose lengthy research papers or cause and effect essays if they already understand those patterns of logic. Embracing students' future goals in the first-year composition classroom can lend itself to the social construction of knowledge—students' abilities to make public what their education and career goals are and how they plan to move forward with their educational process while still in an academic setting. By working with a specific-career focused demographic in sections of writing class, we can shift the focus from our traditional writing expectations to their writing needs.

Background Literature

The 1954 Conference on College Composition and Communication held a workshop to explore the writing processes of college students after completing their required composition course in their freshman year. The report chronicling the events of this workshop notes that: "The members of this workshop began with the assumption that there is a general falling off in composition ability after the freshman year, often to a point where remedial work becomes necessary" (Hackett 114). The findings of this group in 1954 remain constant today. At many universities, students are required to take writing classes within the first year or two of their academic career. Sometimes, depending on the major, students rarely write documents of length for their remaining college days. However, it is not just about enhancing writing across the curriculum (WAC). Perhaps the issue can also be addressed within the composition classroom: If students do not understand practical applications of their composition skills or how to utilize the skills without guidance, we are teaching in a vacuum. We are throwing terminology, skill sets, and expectations at students, knowing that they will need them far beyond the scope of their coursework, but not telling them how or why these skills will be necessary. We need to adjust the coursework to the specific demographics for each field of study, *if not for each individua*l.

In Fragments of Rationality, Lester Faigley identified the shift of composition from a study and response to literature to, well, nothing in particular: "Indeed, the teaching of canonical literature as the primary subject matter for writing courses has diminished considerably since WWII, leaving no single model of writing instruction to replace it" (119). One of the hot topics within composition studies is the role of composition, particularly first-year composition, in the university. Is it a service course? Is it a means of gatekeeping? And, if so, are either of those objectives actually bad? In my experiences as both a professional in student affairs and student services, as well as a faculty member, I find that diverse elements of a college or university are service-oriented: we work in a culture geared to ask, "Would you like a transcript with that?" I do not just believe that composition is a service course because, arguably, a number of general education courses are offered as a service to enrich students' educational and cultural perspectives. Perhaps this is more evident at liberal arts institutions, where a variety of required cultural activities are offered to students as the same kind of service. As much as I myself believe in education for educations' sake, that ideal has drastically changed for many American colleges. Jeff Smith's article "Students' Goals, Gatekeeping, and Some Questions of Ethics" presents the concept of gatekeeping in academics as a natural progression:

> It's obvious that after our students leave our writing classes, most are likely to have to pass through gates: graduation, graduate-school admission, professional certification, job searches, performance and partnership reviews. But even if this weren't so, gatekeeping would still be part of the picture. For students have already passed through gates en route to our classrooms. (303)

Perhaps then, it's the "if you can't beat 'em, join 'em" mentality that I am presenting. I would identify this approach to the writing classroom as a mix of accepting the challenge that Faigley presented of finding a unified model of composition and embracing the unique opportunity of first-year composition as a service course. I cannot convince all of my students of the benefits of the education for educations' sake viewpoint, but I can help them understand and move forward with the career path that they have chosen. I can acknowledge that they have career goals and help them navigate and understand that direction by assisting them to research and develop the genre of writing that they will use in their chosen field of study.

Another consideration for the composition classroom is the overall first-year experience for college students. For anyone who is not familiar with or does not remember college life from the student perspective, Rebekah Nathan (pseudonym) offers a unique perspective on the living and learning situation of *college students* in her book My Freshman Year. Kirk S. Kidwell condenses her experience: "Most will survive their first-year at college and go on to graduate, but all too many will drop out before the freshman year is over" (253). Students are encouraged to take required composition courses in their first (and second, if applicable) semesters as college students. Therefore, while students are in this dramatic transition period, they are also our composition students. Students in our composition courses are "on their way to becoming critical thinkers" (Kidwell 254). They need less guesswork and estimation about their careers and educational paths and more solid, tangible movement towards their individual goals. Students need a composition course with a focus on these individual goals and something to bridge the gap between the information that they learn in school and what they will apply in their careers. For those still struggling to identify the value of higher education, such a shift encourages student buy-in for the educational processes as a whole.

Chris Street and colleagues from the California State University System wrote "The Expository Reading and Writing Curriculum (ERWC): Preparing All Students for College and Career," which also examines the disjointed transition from high school to college-level writing. They begin with the question: "When students have such different needs and goals, how can [the teacher] ensure success for each one of them?" (34). The ERWC is developed from seven principles related to the rhetorical analysis, understanding, and application of texts to both reading and writing. The general nature of these principles allows room to interpret and individualize this learning process for students based on their unique educational and career goals. Karen Bishop Morris's chapter in this collection also explores this concept by asking other difficult questions such as: "Should I penalize an ELL student with strong research writing on a sophisticated idea for making common grammatical errors?" To what end can the process be individualized bearing in mind the ramifications of any decision on the parties involved, both student and faculty?

A specific example of individualizing this process is described in Craig McClure's article "Introducing Scientific Writing to Students Early in Their Academic Careers." This article explores the option of integrating more writing-based activities in an introductory chemistry course to help students understand the writing process as used in their discipline. McClure found that it was "difficult for students late in their undergraduate studies to write in a format appropriate for a scientific journal," which he recognizes as a disservice to the students who will actively pursue a career in the science community (20). In lieu of the incorporation of a WAC program at his institution to systematically guarantee student writing throughout the academic career, McClure has students define sections of a publishable laboratory report. After these sections and subsections are defined, students are required to write in that format for all of the formal writing assignments of the semester. This familiarizes them not only with the writing style but also with the format and language appropriate to their discipline and chosen career path. Though McClure's article specifically describes an activity and writing process for a chemistry major, the concept can be tailored to fit the needs of any academic discipline or a multi-majored composition course. Considering interdisciplinary writing is important for composition faculty and students. Faculty need to ensure that the basics of composition are being taught, but contextualized in a manner that will make writing skills extend across disciplines, as well as outside of college in general.

Pedagogical Implementation

Is there a way to tailor the educational and career writing needs of each student to assignments and coursework in the composition classroom? Is there a way to streamline the process so that students are not working on such individualized projects that it makes grading difficult? Is there a way to blend what we, the composition instructors, want to teach and what the students need to learn? Jonathon Monroe's article "Writing and the Disciplines" identifies the need for instructors to demonstrate the value of writing within various disciplines and model them as a definitive part of each discipline, "not as an add-on or a detour, but as integral to the kinds of research and teaching on which students' success in their respective disciplines necessarily depend" (5). Therefore, it cannot be the goal of the composition instructor to teach the elements of composition or writing that we want to teach; we need to teach what students need to learn.

One of the first assignments that I ask of my face-to-face community college students is to research expectations for writing within their major or career field. This is the first part of a two-part assignment in which students need to identify with their careers and situate themselves within their current field. First, students have to identify what type of writing is used, how it is used, if specific documents are used, if lines just need to be filled in or if independent writing has to be done, what type of language is used, and what is considered appropriate for that genre of writing. For the few students who have not yet declared a major, they have the option to research writing conventions for either their dream jobs or the jobs that they currently hold. Students write a 2–3 page analysis of what they have researched at their own workplace (if they are currently working within their field) or what they have found in online and library inquiry. In the few semesters that I have assigned this type of writing, there have been a wide variety of student responses. Some who actively work in their fields of interests discuss the brief notes that need to be made on medical charts or the terminology used solely by their institution. One student, a criminal justice major, dreams of working for the FBI. His response included documentation of cases, including the importance of recording events as they occur while still maintaining mandated privacy.

The second part of this assignment is for the students to find examples of writing within their field, replicate these documents, and write a reflective analysis about the writing process. Students within the medical fields sometimes choose to find a patient intake form and fill it out, then analyze the type of writing and terminology used. For students who already work within their field, I was hesitant to assign this project for fear that they would already know the answers and not put much time into the assignment. However, I found that students were very engaged in the process. They were receptive to the idea of working within their field and of researching something that directly affects their lives, learning, and career paths.

It became a rewarding experience for these students to see their jobs in a different light. For example, the student who dreams of working for the FBI found official documentation through internet and library research and was able to describe an entire crime scene. This student identified early on that communication and writing are essential for all aspects of accomplishing tasks within the criminal justice field. For instance, the crime scene report could not just read that a dead body was found. All of the necessary elements of narrative-writing had to be enacted: the who, what, where, when, and why. If the writing was lackadaisical, the student learned, the entire investigation could be ruined. These positive revelations are two-fold: the student learns the writing process and the student is able to contextualize the writing process into something that they will need and use in their futures. While it may not be providing a lot of room for student creativity, I feel that that the opportunity for students to work within their fields strongly outweighs my reservations about the direct approach of the assignment.

Once students complete their investigation of writing within their fields, these activities become the basis for several smaller writing-to-learn activities within the classroom. Deanne Gute and Gary Gute identify writing-to-learn activities as those that "require minimal class time and allow instructors to suspend composition and evaluation formalities in order to stimulate deeper engagement" (192). Focusing smaller writing assignments on disciplinary or career-based writing allows students to have a deeper engagement with both the composition course itself and their desired careers. For instance, I have several in-class writing opportunities surrounding the career-based theme including freewriting, letter writing, cover letter writing, and even poetry writing. Allowing students to pay attention to writing within their individualized career paths provides the bigger picture and gives them the opportunity to consider what they will do upon receiving a degree.

The types of writing assignments that I have described do not require that composition instructors become experts in other fields. I do not advocate for composition instructors to learn about crime scene investigation or emergency room incident reports. However, as previously described, the writing process remains the same for all of these genres of writing. Many of the characteristics of traditional genres remain true with the career-based writing. Therefore, the responsibility for investigating disciplines falls onto the student, whereas the instructor remains focused on developing and honing the students' writing process.

Our composition classrooms continuously hold groups of students who, for the most part, do not understand or are not able to connect writing to their personal or professional lives. Though these students rotate through our classrooms at a high volume in a two-year program, it is not our role, as instructors, to teach them just the elements of composition that we like or see value in. We need to actively seek out the type of composition and writing instruction that will be most effective to individual students or demographics of specific fields of study. This reach outside of our own discipline allows for a two-fold advantage: students *learn the* elements of overall good writing, and they learn more about writing as it relates to their career pa*ths. Though the* connotation of service course in relation to composition is usually negative, I advocate for a positive realization of the term in order to embrace the learning opportunities that are best for our students.

Works Cited

Faigley, Lester. *Fragments of Rationality: Postmodernity and the Subject of Composition*. University of Pittsburgh Press, 1992.

Gute, Deanne, and Gute, Gary. "Flow Writing in the Liberal Arts Core and Across the Disciplines: A Vehicle for Confronting and Transforming Academic Disengagement." *The Journal of General Education*, vol. 57, no. 4, 2008, pp. 191–222.

Hackett, Herbert (Workshop Chair). "The Composition Career (of All Students) After the Freshman Year: The Report of Workshop No. 11." *College Composition and Communication*, vol. 5, no. 3, 1954, pp. 114–116.

Kidwell, Kirk S. "Understanding the College First-Year Experience." *The Clearing House*, July/August 2005, pp. 253–255.

McClure, Craig. "Introducing Scientific Writing to Students Early in Their Academic Careers." *Journal of College Science Teaching*, July/August 2009, pp. 20–23.

Monroe, Jonathon. "Writing and the Disciplines." *Peer Review*, Fall 2003, pp. 4–7.

Nathan, Rebekah. *My Freshman Year: What a Professor Learned by Becoming a Student*. Cornell University Press, 2005.

Smith, Jeff. "Students' Goals, Gatekeeping, and Some Questions of Ethics." *College English*, vol. 59, no. 3, 1997, pp. 299–320.

Street, Chris, Jennifer Fletcher, Marcy Merrill, Mira-Lisa Katz, and Zulmara Cline. "The Expository Reading and Writing Curriculum (ERWC): Preparing All Students for College and Career." *The California Reader*, vol. 42, no. 1, 2008, pp. 34–41.

Chapter 17. Confronting the Uncomfortable: Food and First-Year Composition

Matthew Paproth

Georgia Gwinnett College

"Don't get your fuel from the same place your car does."

— *Michael Pollan, Food Rules (57)*

With the popularity of food-related documentaries such as *Super-Size Me* and *Food Inc.*, in conjunction with pivotal texts like Eric Schlosser's *Fast Food Nation* and Michael Pollan's *Omnivore's Dilemma*, food rhetoric has never been more in the public eye. Television has followed suit with popular programs like *Top Chef, Chopped, No Reservations*, and a variety of influential shows on Food Network. In her editorial "What Does It Mean to Write about Food Today?" Evan Kleiman argues that "Writing (and reading) about food has the ability to connect the corporeal, the intellectual and the spiritual worlds we inhabit. That's why food writing is so important now" (465). The mainstream awareness of local, organic, and vegetarian/vegan food movements, primarily as a response to fast food and factory farming, provides an interesting context for college freshmen. Kleiman writes that "How we feed ourselves, in the 21st century in the first world is a choice that has huge moral consequences. For many, the idea that it's a choice may be news" (465). Janet Cramer and Lynn Walters echo this sentiment in the introduction to their book *Food as Communication, Communication as Food*: "Over the last few decades, we have witnessed a rise in food-focused consumption, media, and culture. . . . It seems as if food and the discourses surrounding it, are all over the place, from Jamie Oliver's ventures in American school lunchrooms to news stories about urban gardening or buying organic products at the local farmer's market" (ix).

In recent years, food has become a prevalent topic in college writing courses across the United States. A session at the 2011 College Composition and Communication Conference, *Food for Thought and Action*, proclaimed food issues a part of larger economic, cultural, political and environmental trends, and urged attendees to incorporate food discourse into composition classrooms. Individual presenters shared instructional techniques for food and rhetoric, food blogging inside and outside of the classroom, food and service learning, and food and identity formation (CCCC, 2011). Furthermore, a recent themed issue of *College English* also offers philosophical and pedagogical perspectives on food writing and literature. Lynn Bloom, in addressing the "delectable rhetoric of food writing," describes the genre as "offer[ing] control over at least a small slice of an otherwise refractory world [because it] is most often upbeat and nurturing, providing successes and triumphs—modest and major—for readers to feast on, with occasional glimpses of utopia" (346). Because food stresses abundance, Bloom notes, "Scarcity is not an option," but is instead relegated to the social sciences in fields like politics, history, and sociology. Barbara Waxman extends the discussion to the food memoir which she sees as a "bonding of love and emotion," an expression of cultural identity to people outside a cultural community (363). Waxman situates food memoir in autobiographical theory and the construction of identity which serves to anchor one's self and life. Such a process is a "neurological construction rather than a retrieval operation" (366). Jennifer Cognard-Black and Melissa Goldwaithe also stress the fundamental humanity inherent in food and food writing, asserting that "To teach food as a written art form, is to teach a part of what it means to be human," and they counter negative comments by colleagues who are incredulous that food writing and literature create serious classroom discourse. For Cognard-Black and Goldwaithe, food texts help transmit traditions and history through "Practices of sharing, preparing, and eating recipes [that] help students connect writing and learning to the multiplicities of their own personal food literacies" (422). While most of the writers mentioned above stress the communal aspects of food and how those can be used to engage students in first-year composition courses, I find it useful to push in the opposite direction.

Discomfort Food

One or two young contrarians bravely raise their hands when I ask who in class would try the recipe for stewed dog presented in Jonathan Safran Foer's *Eating Animals*. I even motion toward the door and explain that I have a Crock-Pot of it back in my office. When students begin to shift uncomfortably in their seats, when they begin turning to one another and murmuring things like, "Is he serious?" and one invariably exclaims, "But that's not right!"—then we can begin to delve into the moral and cultural taboos that are broken when we consider eating dogs. Ten or fifteen minutes later, nearly half the class is ready to admit that, in the right situation, they would eat the dog.

Of course the goal here is not to promote the consumption of household pets, but this discussion, which I hold on the first day of my freshman composition course *The Rhetoric of Food* is intended to introduce students to the many unspoken assumptions and decisions that undergird our interaction with food. I strive in my class to make my students more proficient writers, readers, thinkers, and eaters, asking them to consider the various cultural, moral, and political ramifications of the choices that we make regarding food. To do this, I challenge students to embrace the difficult truths and uncomfortable realities that conscious, conscientious eaters face in today's world. In their essay "The Novice as Expert: Writing the Freshman Year," Nancy Sommers and Laura Saltz discuss the importance of challenging students in freshman writing classes to "build authority not by writing *from* a position of expertise but by writing *into* expertise" (134). They discuss the importance of using the course as a threshold: "Thresholds, of course, are dangerous places. Students are asked as freshmen to leave something behind and to locate themselves in the realms of uncertainty and ambiguity. It doesn't take long for most first-year students to become aware of the different expectations between high school and college writing, that something more is being offered to them and, at the same time, asked of them" (125). Rather than shying away from the uncertainty and discomfort associated with this approach, I embrace it in my choice of discussion topics, writing assignments, and course texts.

What's at Steak? (groan)

For most college students, eating is a perilous activity. Traditional college students have either just left home and moved into a dorm—left to fend for themselves with choices limited to fast food, not-much-better-cafeteria food, or whatever they can cook on their probably-illegal hotplate—or are still living at home and eating whatever their parents serve them. Non-traditional college students have more freedom but less time, and, for most of the students I have taught, there is a willful neglect of eating healthily or ethically in favor of food handed to them through a window and finished before they arrive home. For my students, the economic realities of eating are perhaps the least comfortable, as eating ethically and organically is something that most people cannot afford to do.

In teaching multiple iterations of this course over the past few years, I have been continually surprised by the wide range of experiences and perspectives that arise during class discussion. When I asked one student, who had decided to try vegetarianism for a ten-week class project, how she planned to accomplish this potentially difficult goal, she replied, "I'll just eat a lot of chicken." However, for every response like this one, I encounter another student who is well aware of the problems posed by factory farming and fast food industries. I have taught students who grew up on small farms and eat only animals raised in those environments, hunters who have thought a great deal about the ethical implications of eating meat, and fast food workers who bring incredible anecdotal evidence supporting claims made in course readings.

Keeping the course objectives of the freshman composition sequence in mind is an important part in conceptualizing the course. I am conscious of not proselytizing for local and organic food to my students, though it is often tempting to do so. Teaching students to eat right, as important as it is, unfortunately is not an outcome of first-year communication courses. The struggle is to balance this ethical dimension of the class with the more relevant outcomes of teaching the principles of logical argument, critical reading, and effective writing.

Critical Reading

For the course texts, I choose readings that are confrontational about how and why we make decisions about what we eat. For example, Michael Pollan's "Out of the Kitchen, Onto the Couch" discusses the inverse correlation between the time we spend cooking and the time we spend watching people cook on television. I have also used Safran Foer's *Eating Animals*, Eric Schlosser's *Fast Food Nation*, and Pollan's *Omnivore's Dilemma* to demonstrate how to create larger arguments that approach the similar topics from drastically different perspectives.

David Foster Wallace's essay "Consider the Lobster" is perhaps the quintessential text for a course on discomfort food. Originally written for *Gourmet* magazine, the piece begins as a narrative of Foster Wallace's experience at the Maine Lobster Festival. In these pages, Foster Wallace describes the bacchanalian experience of attending the massive festival. However, midway through the lengthy essay, he addresses his growing concern—"So then here is a question that's all but unavoidable at the World's Largest Lobster Cooker, and may arise in kitchens across the U.S.: Is it all right to boil a sentient creature alive just for our gustatory pleasure?" (243). From this point onward, the essay turns into a discussion of complex questions that we often eschew:

> The more important point here, though, is that the whole animal-cruelty-and-eating issue is not just complex, it's also uncomfortable. It is, at any rate, uncomfortable for me, and for just about everyone I know who enjoys a variety of foods and yet does not want to see herself as cruel or unfeeling. As far as I can tell, my own main way of dealing with this conflict has been to avoid thinking about the whole unpleasant thing. (Wallace 246)

The publication of this controversial piece in *Gourmet* provides an opportunity for students to think about audience; furthermore, Foster Wallace's structurally elegant rendering of this moral dilemma provides a model for developing writers of how to weave narrative and analytical discourse together in a satisfying way.

Discussions and Assignments

Early class discussions negotiate the various types of guilt that we feel as eaters— guilt about eating too much food, about eating overly processed foods, about having food while people in other countries do not, about eating other living creatures, about not caring or thinking enough about our food choices. As students become more informed about and engaged in the rhetoric of eating, they begin to gravitate toward the ideas and concepts that are the most important and/or relevant to them. Many of these discussions are deeply uncomfortable for students, as they begin to realize the deeply troubling nature of the industrial farming complex and the near impossibility of removing themselves from it. We talk at length about what and why they are affected by these readings, which provides a context for discussing ethos, pathos, and logos. Students become adept at recognizing when various appeals are being used, and how they are being used by different authors at different times. For some students, the notion of animal pain and suffering strikes the hardest; for others, fear of becoming sick (we spend an inordinate amount of time discussing what Safran Foer dubs *fecal soup* in industrial chickens) weighs the heaviest. Some find themselves enthralled by stories of midnight trips to factory farms or attempts to track a single cow from birth to burger; others are more convinced by the sheer numbers and vastness of the systems.

Although students respond to these discussions in a variety of ways, it is interesting to see a small number invariably set about trying to poke holes in arguments for vegetarianism or against factory farming: "If everyone stopped eating meat, what would happen to the animals? And the jobs?" or perhaps "That chicken is already dead by the time it gets to the grocery store—there's nothing to do with it at that point." These completely understandable reactions provide amazing opportunities to demonstrate how arguments are structured (more often than not, they point us to a discussion of rhetorical fallacies), and they lead students to identify the areas of food rhetoric that matter to them.

These interests manifest themselves in the central project for the course, an electronic food journal; a few weeks into class, students begin this assignment, which asks them to set specific food-related goals for themselves and then track them over the course of ten weeks. In subsequent weeks, they respond to prompts that are aligned with course readings and other course assignments. One prompt asks them to interview people in their lives; another asks them to keep extensive notes of what they eat throughout the week, identifying what, where, why, and how much they eat; another asks them to prepare a recipe and chronicle the experience for their readers. The larger goal of the project is to allow students to develop ideas and set goals that they strive toward over a period of time, interacting with each other, course texts, and the outside world to arrive at a better understanding of their place in the food system.

I echo these goals in a service-learning project that I try to incorporate into the structure of the course. Given the nature of the course, it is important that students communicate some of what we have discussed in class to the outside world. Although I have handled this differently in various iterations of the course, at some point I always direct students outward. In the past, this has manifested itself in interviews with family members, school administrators, and people in the food service and food production industries. Other projects have asked students to compose and send letters to members of the community in which they solicited information, made recommendations, and proposed solutions to food-related problems. The service-learning aspects of the course provide students the opportunity to communicate what they have learned in the real world, with real consequences and to real people, which pulls together many of the predominant issues recurring throughout the course.

Thanksgiving: The Final Exam

Especially when I teach the course in the fall semester, Thanksgiving looms ominously in the distance for most of my students. In the final chapter of *Eating Animals*, Safran Foer argues that "The Thanksgiving turkey embodies the paradoxes of eating animals: what we do to living turkeys is just about as bad as anything humans have ever done to any animal in the history of the world. Yet what we do with their dead bodies can feel so powerfully good and right" (249). For many of my students, it provides a litmus test as to their feelings moving into the future about eating meat and eating ethically. In the final entry of their food journals, I ask students to consider how the class has changed their view of Thanksgiving.

In the final weeks of the course, I shift the focus and the tone toward things that we can do, steps that we can take to be more comfortable in our interaction with food. The final course reading is Michael Pollan's *Food Rules*, which lays out (in easy-to-read pamphlet form) a set of 64 steps that we *can* take, foods that we *should* eat, and ways that we can survive in today's world. The final assignment is an oral presentation where students explain a few of Pollan's rules and demonstrate them through visual and edible aids. I stress the importance of engaging thoughtfully with any food being served to the class; by making the food demonstrable evidence of the rules in Pollan's book, students are impelled to enact the principles learned throughout the course. While it may not be easy—for students, the logistics of preparing and serving food can be overwhelming—the class ends by eating food, prepared with thought and care by people who, months earlier, may not have even known that chicken was considered meat.

Conclusion

Everybody eats. As a first-year composition theme, food inherently appeals to students across political, socioeconomic, racial, and gender boundaries. However an instructor approaches the course, writing and talking about food in the space of the first-year composition classroom provides students with a safe space and bountiful opportunities to consider the questions and assumptions that underpin our everyday relationship with the foods we eat. In ways that are comfortable, uncomfortable, or both, students learn to read, write, speak, and think critically about how what we eat defines who we are.

Works Cited

Bloom, Lynn Z. "Consuming Prose: The Delectable Rhetoric of Food Writing." *College English*, vol. 70, no. 4, 2008, pp. 346–362.

Cognard-Black, Jennifer, and Melissa A. Goldthwaite. "Books That Cook: Teaching Food and Food Literature in the English Classroom." *College English*, vol. 70, no. 4, 2008, pp. 421–436.

Cramer, Janet M., Carlnita P. Greene, and Lynn M. Walters. *Food as Communication, Communication as Food*. Peter Lang, 2011.

Foster Wallace, David. *Consider the Lobster and Other Essays*. Back Bay, 2007.

Kleiman, Evan. "What Does It Mean to Write About Food Today?" *Journal of Sustainable Agriculture*, vol. 35, no. 5, 2011, pp. 465–466.

Pollan, Michael. *Food Rules: An Eater's Manual*. Penguin, 2009.

———. *Omnivore's Dilemma*. Penguin, 2006.

Safran Foer, Jonathan. *Eating Animals*. Back Bay, 2010.

Sommers, Nancy, and Laura Saltz. "The Novice as Expert: Writing the Freshman Year." *College Composition and Communication*, vol. 56, no. 1, 2004, pp. 124–149.

Waxman, Barbara Frey. "Food Memoirs: What They Are, Why They Are Popular, and Why They Belong in the Literature Classroom." *College English*, vol. 70, no. 4, 2008, pp. 363–383.

Contributors

Sean Barnette is Associate Professor in the Department of English and Foreign Languages at Lander University in Greenwood, SC, where he teaches first-year writing, linguistics, and rhetoric. He also serves as the internship coordinator for English majors and as a teacher and advisor within Lander's Honors College.

Lori Brown is a former high school German teacher, assistant principal and school district grant writer who currently works as Director of Learning Solutions and Services at ASCD. Working from her home in Asheville, N.C., Brown continues to publish in both the academic and faith-based sector, holding degrees in German and educational leadership from Davidson College, Furman University, and Western Carolina University. Her doctoral research focused on teacher response to the violent writings of secondary students.

Lillian Craton is Associate Professor of English at Lander University in South Carolina, as well as Director of the Honors College. While her primary research area is British literature, particularly Victorian studies, she teaches composition every semester and is deeply passionate about the work of mentoring student writers.

Kathryn Crowther is Assistant Professor of English at Georgia State University's Perimeter College, where she teaches first-year composition and British literature. In addition to her research on teaching and learning, she specializes in nineteenth-century British literature, contemporary Neo-Victorian literature, and Steampunk, and she is also pursuing research in disability studies, autism and literature, and digital pedagogy.

Casie Fedukovich, is Assistant Professor in English and serves at the Associate Director of the First-Year Writing Program at North Carolina State University. Her research explores graduate teacher training, most recently in the context of disability studies, and writing program administration.

Rachel Anya Fomalhaut is an adjunct professor of writing, English, and women's, gender, and sexuality studies at Ithaca College, Elmira College, and Binghamton University, all in upstate New York. Her dissertation, "The Affective Representation of Loss in Multi-Cultural Women's Literature," contains a chapter on writing pedagogy focused on FYC and WAC/WID.

Lynée Lewis Gaillet is Professor and Chair of the English department at Georgia State University. She has published numerous articles and books addressing Scottish rhetoric, writing program administration, composition/rhetoric history and pedagogy, publishing matters, and archival research methods.

Christopher Garland received his Ph.D. from the University of Florida and is Assistant Professor in the Department of English at the University of Southern Mississippi. His most recent publications are in the journals *Social and Economic*

Studies, Contemporary French and Francophone Studies, and *Writing Visual Culture*. He is currently at work on his first book.

Ruth A. Goldfine is Professor of English and Interim Associate Dean of University College at Kennesaw State University in Kennesaw, Georgia. Her research focuses on her work with first-year students (both in English composition courses and in first-year seminar classes) and in the area of the scholarship of teaching and learning.

Pamela Henney serves as Adjunct Instructor of English at Kent State University in Kent, OH, and North Central State College in Mansfield, OH. Her research focuses on varied approaches to assisting first-year composition students to become successful writers, academic and beyond.

Renée Love is Dean of Arts & Humanities at Lander University, a regional, public university in SC. She is also Associate Professor of English and a columnist; her scholarship often includes topics related to student success, civic rhetoric, faculty development, and human potential.

Rachel McCoppin is Professor of Literature at the University of Minnesota-Crookston. She has published scholarly articles in the areas of mythology and comparative literature. She has also published the books, *The Lessons of Nature in Mythology* (McFarland 2015) and *The Hero's Journey and the Cycles of Nature* (McFarland 2016).

Deborah Mixson-Brookshire serves as Assistant Dean, Director of Distance Learning, and Associate Professor of Management in University College at Kennesaw State University in Kennesaw, Georgia. The majority of her research efforts and publications focus on first-year students and strategies that facilitate their academic success, such as experiential education and distance learning.

Karen Bishop Morris is Associate Professor, Director of First-Year Writing, and Director of the Calumet Campus Writing Center at Purdue University Northwest. Her work has appeared in *English Education*, *WPA: The Journal for Writing Program Administrators*, and several edited collections.

Sarah O'Connor serves as Professor in the School of Writing, Rhetoric and Technical Communication at James Madison University in Harrisonburg, Virginia, where she teaches both graduate and undergraduate courses. She is also the co-director of the Humanitarian Affairs minor and the JMU in LA program.

Matt Paproth is currently Assistant Professor of English at Georgia Gwinnett College, where he teaches courses in contemporary British literature, digital media, first-year composition, and developmental writing. He received his Ph.D. from Southern Illinois University Carbondale and worked as a Marion L. Brittain Postdoctoral Fellow at the Georgia Institute of Technology. He has published essays on contemporary television, digital pedagogy, and postmodernist fiction. His thematic composition courses have covered diverse topics such as writing rock and roll, eating ethically, postmodernist revisions of *Robinson Crusoe*, time and *Breaking Bad*, and digital mapping and *Ulysses*.

Abigail G. Scheg is a course mentor for General Education Composition at Western Governors University. She researches, writes, publishes, and conferences in the areas of online pedagogy, educational technology, composition, and popular culture.

Lisa Whalen teaches writing and literature at North Hennepin Community College in Brooklyn Park, Minnesota.